*[handwritten signatures]*

Kevin D. H__

Carolyn Swiszcz

# BETTER POLITICS, PLEASE

## 35 STORIES OF POLITICIANS WHO VALUE HOPE OVER HATE

### BY KEVIN D. HENDRICKS

### ILLUSTRATED BY CAROLYN SWISZCZ

D0711963

Published by Monkey Outta Nowhere

West St. Paul, Minnesota

MonkeyOuttaNowhere.com

KevinDHendricks.com

Copyright © 2020 Kevin D. Hendricks

Cover design by Darci Read

Illustrations by Carolyn Swiszcz

ISBN: 9798676180379

To my grandma, Wanda Madden.

# TABLE OF CONTENTS

Introduction...................................................... 9

A Word About Perfection ............................................ 17

Profiles ........................................................... 19

- N.J. Akbar: "Giving up is not an option.".. 20

- Quotes: George Washington ......................... 23

- Justin Amash: "Most members of
  Congress don't think anymore." ................... 24

- Bushra Amiwala:
  "Good things are sure to happen." ............. 29

- Two Retiring Senators in Oregon:
  "I miss working with the Republicans.".......32

- Quotes: John F. Kennedy ................................ 35

- Charlie Baker: "Let's make our brand
  of politics positive and optimistic." ............. 37

- Three Teen Candidates in Kansas:
  "I may not be the victor, but I can be
  the influencer." .................................................. 40

- Cory Booker: "We need a revival of
  civic grace." ........................................................ 42

- Quotes: Peggy Noonan .................................... 47

- Ruth Buffalo: "I was never raised to
  see party lines." ................................................ 48

- G.T. Bynum: "Doing the right thing is not always popular."............................51

- Dan Crenshaw: "Just be part of the solution." ...............................................54

- Quotes: Madeleine Albright...........................58

- Carlos Curbelo: "I want to get something done."...............................................59

- Tammy Duckworth: "It's never going to be as bad as getting blown up." ....................63

- Maia Espinoza: "People are really looking for that message of hope."..............................66

- Quotes: Susan Collins .......................................70

- Beth Fukumoto: "But do it with kindness." ...................................71

- Justin Giboney: "If we can't have conversations then we can't have a good democracy."...............................................75

- Jenean Hampton: "I just wanted to help make Kentucky better."..........................86

- Caleb Hanna: "Politics affect everything you care about."...............................................83

- Jaime Herrera Beutler: "If you spend all your time sowing discord, that's what you're going to reap."......................................................86

- Adam Kinzinger: "What can we solve today?" .......................................................89

- Quotes: Franklin Roosevelt ............................ 92

- Brenda Kupchick:
  "Progress over politics." .................................... 93

- Cassandra Levesque:
  "We are unstoppable." ..................................... 96

- Quotes: Ronald Reagan ................................... 99

- Jeff Lunde: "We're so diverse we have
  a Republican mayor." ...................................... 100

- Quotes: Abraham Lincoln ............................. 103

- Matt Little: "We will never heal our
  democracy hiding behind a keyboard." ... 105

- Quotes: Hillary Clinton .................................. 108

- Lisa Murkowski: "Consensus should
  not be a dirty word." ....................................... 109

- Svante Myrick: "I could dork out over
  sidewalk legislation." ..................................... 115

- Quotes: John McCain ...................................... 119

- Collin Peterson: "We've wasted money
  on stupider things." ........................................ 120

- Jared Polis: "We are better together." ...... 124

- Quotes: Barack Obama ................................... 126

- Qasim Rashid: "The bigger risk is for
  me to stay silent." ........................................... 129

- Regina Romero: "Whoever you voted for— let's work together!".........................133

- Max Rose: "We get shit done."....................137

- Quotes: John F. Kennedy...............................141

- Ben Sasse: "Start from the assumption that our opponents are like us." .................142

- Hillary Schieve: "Don't tell me we can't find something in common.".........................146

- Pat Spearman: "Equality is breaking out all over the world."..............................149

- Quotes: Fannie Lou Hamer ...........................152

- Elise Stefanik: "If you're willing to lead, people will support you.".................................153

- Erin Stewart: "We can disagree without being disagreeable." .........................................157

- Quotes: John Lewis.........................................160

What's Next...................................................................161

About the Author .........................................................170

About the Illustrator....................................................171

Acknowledgments.......................................................172

Notes ...........................................................................177

# INTRODUCTION

"So who are you voting for?"

That's the question my grandma asks in the middle of dinner when I visit family. It catches me off guard every time.

My grandma doesn't normally talk politics. She's a quiet farm wife who loves deeply and always seems to avoid conflict.

But almost every time I visit, she'll ask who I'm voting for or what I think about what's going on in the world. Lately she'd ask what I think about Donald Trump. (And my mom audibly sighs.)

I always pause for a minute before answering, never sure if we are really going to talk politics. But I realized my grandma doesn't ask in order to start a debate. She asks because she cares what I think. It isn't about changing my mind or pushing a specific issue. She cares about me and no political disagreement could get in the way.

That should be a simple thing, but it's pretty rare these days.

## WE THE PEOPLE

Too often, politics feels like a battleground where we lob accusations back and forth. Both sides are firmly entrenched, not willing to give any ground. The other side is the enemy, wrong no matter what, and we will defeat them.

That's not likely to change after November's presidential election, no matter who wins or loses.

Politics have long been divisive, and people will always disagree. But I have hope that we can do better.

If only because it's not supposed to be a battle ground. It's not us vs. them, it's we the people.

If we want to make civic engagement civil, that's where it needs to start.

It starts with caring for one another, like my grandma. We have to look for the best in each other, instead of always looking for how to win an argument. There has to be a willingness to find common ground—and that's never easy, because common ground is rarely safe or comfortable.

## *WHAT DOES IT REALLY MEAN?*

It's one thing to talk about common ground in a vague sense, but how does that actually work when we talk about real people and real positions?

- Will Republicans be horrified I'm writing about North Dakota's Ruth Buffalo, a Native American woman who unseated the author of a voter ID bill and quickly drew comparisons to "The

Squad"?

- Will Democrats be horrified I'm writing about Jaime Herrera Beutler, an anti-abortion advocate who called the impeachment process a "goat rodeo"?

It's not always comfortable trying to find something to celebrate in people you disagree with. But it is possible.

- I hope anyone could be inspired by Herrera Beutler's story of her daughter's survival against the odds and would applaud her work to fight maternal mortality.

- Likewise, I hope anyone could be inspired by Buffalo's story of running for her children and the next generation—not the false narrative that she set out to defeat the author of the voter ID bill in some kind of liberal vendetta.

Better politics doesn't mean we all hold hands and sing together. But it does mean we step off the battlefield and see one another as fellow Americans.

Sometimes that's hard work.

While writing the profile of Republican Congressman Adam Kinzinger, I had some doubts. I browsed through his social media feed and saw him refer to the "radical left." None of the people I profile are going to be perfectly bipartisan (more on that later), but I felt discouraged that he was using that kind of divisive language.

Then I came across a video Kinzinger made about conspiracy theories and COVID-19. He didn't demonize or
blame. He inspired and encouraged. He talked about
how and why these conspiracies are dividing us and
urged us to "unplug the rage machine."

Regardless of how I felt about every one of Kinzinger's
positions or his social media rhetoric, that was a video
I could get behind.

Politics will never be simple and easy. We'll always
find ways to disagree. But if we can find that one bit
of common ground where we agree, I think that can
make all the difference. It doesn't solve everything
and we still disagree on a lot, but it unplugs the rage
machine, as Kinzinger put it, and makes things a little
more sane.

Those are the stories I share in this book. For almost
every profile there was a moment when I saw them
offer a glimmer of better politics. It was never about a
certain stance on a political issue.

It was a moment when I saw them as an authentic,
messy human:

- For Republican Congressman Dan Crenshaw—a gruff character if there ever was one—
  it was his appearance on *Saturday Night Live*
  to accept an apology for a joke about his eye
  patch.

- For Democratic Senator Cory Booker, it was

his refusal to throw Republican Senator Rand Paul under the bus despite the urging of late-night host Stephen Colbert.

- For Tea Party conservative and former Kentucky Lieutenant Governor Jenean Hampton, it was the family rift over politics.

- For Tucson Mayor Regina Romero, a Democrat who supports immigrant rights, it was her opposition to a sanctuary city ballot proposal that caught my eye.

Every one of these stories is centered not so much on the issues but how we approach the issues. You might disagree with where some of these politicians stand (I sure do!), but a specific political stance isn't the point. It's how we advocate and whether or not we're willing to see past disagreements to how we can work together.

## WHY DID YOU PICK THAT PERSON?!

There are some people in this book I didn't want to write about. I disagree with them, but more than that, their style or their delivery or their arrogance drives me nuts. But part of better politics is setting differences aside and finding things we can agree on.

I don't expect you to like every person this project

profiles. But I do hope you'll understand them a little better and see them as human. That doesn't mean you vote for them, but maybe it means you don't hate them.

And let's be honest: Sometimes the divide is too far. Sometimes people are too entrenched, and issues are too divisive to find any common ground. Sometimes there are issues where we won't—and shouldn't—compromise.

But as we sit down and talk to each other, as we look for something we can agree on, the hope is the gap isn't as far as we think it is. The hope is that common ground isn't as rare as we think.

# CUT THROUGH THE SHENANIGANS

Rock star and idealist Bono of U2 has always said that compromise isn't a dirty word. He famously worked with President George W. Bush on fighting HIV/AIDS. While there are many areas where Bono and Bush might disagree, they were able to find common ground in this one area.

During an interview on *The Today Show,* co-host Jenna Bush Hager—the former president's daughter—asked, "Do you remember the first time you met my dad?"

"Yeah, well, he didn't want to see me, which is fair

enough," Bono recalled. "Different political views and whatever."

A classic bit of understatement from the rock and roll showman before he got serious: "I think we've got to cut through the shenanigans of political cartooning and see that some people can have different views and still be principled people," Bono said.

That's better politics. Seeing past our divergent views and caring about the person. Bono did it with George W. Bush. My grandma did it with me. And it's time 'we the people' do that for each other.

# A WORD ABOUT PERFECTION

One of my greatest worries in writing this book is what happens when someone I profile acts like a jerk or does something that's the opposite of finding common ground?

Well, that's going to happen. These are still politicians who want to get elected and will do partisan things.

As I write these profiles of politicians, it's very clear to me that they are still people. I'm not highlighting heroes for us to worship no matter what, I'm featuring imperfect people. Many of the people profiled will let us down. I suspect they'll make statements or support legislation or do something that is not in line with better politics.

When that happens, the solution isn't to rip them out of the book and never speak of them again. The solution is to realize they are human. They've probably already done something that's not exactly better politics.

While writing this book I actually researched and wrote a profile of a state legislator who seemed to fit the bill of common ground. He talked about bringing people together and getting things accomplished. He contrasted the gridlock of Washington, D.C., with his state's progress and highlighted the importance of letting people have a voice in the process and not catering to the extreme voices. It was a great story.

Turns out he lied.

A whole scandal came to light where he met with one of the extreme lobbyists he'd decried, badmouthed his fellow legislators, and struck a deal to come after legislators in the election, something he'd promised not to do. The calls for his resignation were fierce, and though he didn't resign, he's not running for re-election in 2020. A political career of more than 20 years came to a crashing halt.

So yeah, the folks in this book might disappoint us. But my hope is we can find something to celebrate, despite those eventual disappointments.

# PROFILES

# N.J. AKBAR

## "GIVING UP IS NOT AN OPTION."

"I ran because I want to make sure that there's some-one on our school board who understands what it's like to succeed in education, but also knows what it's like to struggle," N.J. Akbar said in a WKYC story. Ak-bar is the first openly LGBTQ Muslim elected in Ohio and serves as the vice president of the Akron School Board. He works as the assistant dean of University College at Kent State University. Akbar is also an Army veteran.

For the success he's experienced today, he's had more than his share of struggle.

"I saw drugs all around me," said Akbar. "I saw alcohol-ism, I saw poverty. I didn't see a lot of success." Akbar went into third grade barely able to read and was sent to special education classes.

"But he had that spark in his eye that told me he want-ed to be there," said his third-grade teacher, Michele Deacon.

Deacon represented a turning point for Akbar.

"When I met Ms. Deacon, it kind of really put me on this path of loving school," said Akbar. "She was just very patient and caring, took extra time and it made me love reading. I don't think without her I would have a Ph.D. now."

In 2017, Akbar had a failed run for school board and also lost his mother. In the resulting depression, he almost gave up on his doctorate program.

"My mother passed away in 2017, and you know I almost quit the program because I just went into a deep depression," said Akbar. "In that depression I sent an email to my adviser and told her I was quitting."

But his advisor talked him out of it.

"I've always learned through my failures," said Akbar. "I always analyze what is it that I could do better. How do I come out stronger so that they never are able to beat me again?"

Not only did Akbar get his doctorate, but he also ran for school board again.

"I found myself at a crossroads with the vitriolic sentiment overtaking our politics," Akbar said in a Medium piece. "I believe that all politics are local and began asking my friends to run for office. One turned it back onto me and asked for the reason I was not considering a run myself."

"I decided I was who my community needed as a member of our Board of Education," Akbar said.

He's helped lead the Akron School Board through the

COVID-19 crisis and has helped increase transparency and address institutional racism.

For Akbar, it's important to involve others: "We ask the same leaders to do everything," he told the *Beacon Journal.*

"Run," Akbar said. "Do not let others define you or pigeonhole you into one box."

In 2020, Akbar gave a virtual commencement speech at one of Akron's high schools, urging graduates to make the most of their moment.

"Today will forever be etched in your memories as one of your moments," Akbar said. "Enjoy it. But do not rest. There are moments like this one ahead. Moments where you will be unequivocally requested to rise to the occasion. To make a memory. To make history. To do something that has never been done before.

"As you make those moments, never for a second believe that you are not deserving to be there. Or that you're not prepared. I'm here to tell you that you are more than prepared and that you are more than enough.

"Let this moment show you that giving up is not an option. That you will succeed, that you will overcome, that you will realize your dreams."

"Towards the preservation of your government, and the permanency of your present happy state, it is requisite, not only that you steadily discountenance irregular oppositions to its acknowledged authority, but also that you resist with care the spirit of innovation upon its principles, however specious the pretexts."

**—PRESIDENT GEORGE WASHINGTON IN HIS FAREWELL ADDRESS ON SEPT. 19, 1796**

# JUSTIN AMASH

## "MOST MEMBERS OF CONGRESS DON'T THINK ANYMORE."

In 2020, Democrats heralded Michigan Representative Justin Amash for crossing the aisle to vote to impeach President Donald Trump.

"I rise today in support of these articles of impeachment," Amash said in his speech from the House floor. "I come to this floor not as a Democrat, not as a Republican, but as an American who cares deeply about the Constitution, the rule of law, and the rights of the people under our system of government."

Amash, a former Republican first elected in the Tea Party wave of 2010, left the Republican Party in 2019. But rather than the beginning of a bipartisan push, Amash was the sole non-Democrat vote in the House.

"Modern politics is trapped in a partisan death spiral," Amash wrote in a *Washington Post* op-ed announcing his departure. "No matter your circumstances, I'm asking you to join me in rejecting the partisan loyalties and rhetoric that divide and dehumanize us. I'm asking you to believe that we can do better than this two-party system—and to work toward it. If we continue to take America for granted, we will lose it."

And far from a moderate Republican who could cross over to be a Blue Dog Democrat, Amash actually distanced himself from Republicans by being even more conservative. He joined the Libertarian Party in 2020. He even considered running for president with the Libertarian Party, but ultimately decided against it.

"Americans are ready for practical approaches based in humility and trust of the people," he said in a CNN story on his presidential hopes. "We're ready for a presidency that will restore respect for our Constitution and bring people together."

Amash's willingness to buck the parties has led to some frank and honest critiques of Congress.

"It's very freeing to not feel bound to a particular party," Amash said in an article from The Hill.

Amash has called out:

- **The stranglehold party leadership has on members:** "On ordinary legislative matters, most members of Congress don't think anymore," he told *RollingStone*. "They just follow whatever they're told by their leadership."

- **The broken process:** "Congress doesn't legislate. What you see on TV is theater," he said on Twitter. "Dem and GOP leaders aren't interested in addressing problems; they're interested in messaging about problems. The real work of legislating is hard. It's simpler and more politically beneficial to put on a show," he tweeted.

- **The hypocrisy of Congress:** "We've witnessed members of Congress from both parties shift their views 180 degrees—on the importance of character, on the principles of obstruction of justice—depending on whether they're discussing Bill Clinton or Donald Trump," Amash said on Twitter in response to the Mueller report.

Amash argues that Congress is so dysfunctional that good friends pretend to be enemies.

"You could see two people who are so hostile to each other, two representatives, two senators, but actually they're friends," Amash said on the Free Thoughts podcast. "But on TV they're enemies, on Twitter they're enemies, and you don't even know it."

"AOC is a good example," Amash continued. "She has a good relationship with many, many members of Congress and many Republicans but you'd never know it. In person, she's actually a person that gets along with people. But you wouldn't know it based on the way people react to her on Twitter or on TV, these same people who behind the scenes might be friends with her will say vicious things. And I mean, personal things."

"It's fine to disagree on policy. I disagree with her on many, many policies," Amash said. "But it's so strange to me for someone to be that two-faced where they will be kind to someone in person, but then go on TV and say horrible things. ... Just because you're friends with someone doesn't mean you have to agree with them on the policies. I have lots of friends on both sides of the aisle, who I don't agree with on policies, but we're good friends."

For Amash, the dysfunction ultimately comes down to the two-party system. He points to George Washington's warning about political parties.

"Because Congress is so focused on this team mentality, team red versus team blue, that trickles back down to society, and you see the same thing back home," Amash said. "And then they see people back home thinking team red versus team blue, and then that trickles back up. It's a feedback loop and nobody's able to break out of it."

Unfortunately, Amash doesn't have a lot of optimism in the short term.

"I don't think you're going to change that anytime soon," he said. "I don't think you're going to get rid of Trumpism anytime soon. I joined the Libertarian party because I think that in the next decade or so there needs to be a strong opposition through a political party. I want a future where everyone is an independent. Where you don't have to have party labels, but I think that is more of a long-term thing."

Amash may not have optimism in the system—he opted not to run for re-election in 2020—but one thing does give him hope.

"Actually, most Americans are delightful people, are polite people, want to work with each other, respect each other," Amash said in a *Newsweek* article.

# BUSHRA AMIWALA

## "GOOD THINGS ARE SURE TO HAPPEN."

"I lost my election in March, but I still made history," Bushra Amiwala wrote for *Glamour*. "I registered more than 2,000 people to vote, and 30% of my votes came from people who voted for the first time."

Amiwala made headlines in her losing campaign for the Cook County Board of Commissioners in 2018. At the time she was a 19-year-old college student.

She thought she might be done in politics, but her opponent asked to meet with her and over breakfast told her she should run for public office again. Six months later she ran for school board and won, becoming the youngest Muslim elected to public office in the country.

"Not only did he support me, but he also contributed to my campaigns and was only just a phone call away," Amiwala said in an interview with *14East* magazine. "He wasn't the only one who was asking me to run for the board. A lot of parents, and former board members, board presidents, Skokie elected officials, trustees... I think all of them saw something in me that I didn't see in myself at the time and that's what inspired me to run."

Amiwala has a habit of taking inspiration from her opponents. In 2016 she interned for Republican Senator Mark Kirk, because as a Democrat she wanted to better understand the other side.

"I thought going into it that all Republicans were evil and mean," Amiwala said in a Brown Political Review interview. "However, all of those were challenged right off the bat and I was really pleasantly surprised by the amount of friends that I made on the Kirk campaign and how nice everyone was to me."

Amiwala learned a lot from that experience, including that bipartisanship only goes so far. A staffer encouraged Amiwala to run for office. When she finally decided to do it, they weren't quite as helpful as she hoped.

"A couple of months later, I called the senator's office back and said 'Yes, I want to run, will you all support me?'" she told *Seventeen*. "They basically said, 'Hell no! You're running as a Democrat!' I was like, 'Oh shoot, true,' which shows how naive I was at the time."

But Amiwala has turned that naivety into hard-won experience.

"No matter what happens in the election, I've been able to show people that if your heart's in the right place, you're working toward making a difference, and you're fighting for the right causes and a positive change, you'll see the results in one way or another,"

Amiwala said. "Everyone has power, whether it's in our voices or in our actions—just use it for good, and good things are sure to happen."

# TWO RETIRING SENATORS IN OREGON

## "I MISS WORKING WITH THE REPUBLICANS."

Even with majorities in both houses of the Oregon Legislature in 2019, Democrats still have to work with Republicans. That became painfully clear when Republican senators walked out of negotiations on a cap and trade climate bill, denying Democrats a quorum and leaving them unable to pass the measure.

"The saddest thing I've seen happen over the 12 years I've been at the statehouse is the steady erosion of bipartisanship," said State Senator Cliff Bentz, a Republican, in a *Mail Tribune* story. "And it's one of the reasons I'm leaving."

"We are becoming more fractured even within our own caucus," said State Senator Laurie Monnes Anderson, a Democrat. "I miss working with the Republicans."

It turns out Monnes Anderson is part of that fracture. She joined two other Democrats in refusing to support the climate bill, killing it much more effectively than the Republican walkout. She took a lot of heat for that action, but she wanted to see improvements to the bill that just weren't there. But that heat won't come from voters as Monnes Anderson decided not to run for re-election.

"I'd made the decision before the real divisive session last [time]," Monnes Anderson said. "But that's certainly something that I don't like. It's not me. It's not my personality. I like bringing people together and trying to work out a solution."

Bentz also wanted a solution, participating in an all-day, marathon session with Democratic Governor Kate Brown looking for a compromise that ultimately didn't materialize. Then the Republicans walked out—and they didn't just walk out, they left the state after Governor Brown instructed the Oregon State Patrol to bring the senators back to the capitol.

"The tactic is not unknown to the governor," Bentz said in an *Argus-Observer* article, pointing to previous walkouts by Democrats, including Brown. In fact, walkouts aren't unique in Oregon politics. Republicans did it twice in 2019 and once so far in 2020, but Democrats have done it in 2001, 1995, and 1971. Apparently Abraham Lincoln himself once jumped out a window in an attempt to deny quorum (it failed).

"Let me just say, I wish we didn't have to walk out," said Bentz. "It's not something I thought I would ever have to do, but the damage that House Bill 2020 will do to Oregon, in general, and to Ontario and Malheur

County, specifically, is so long term, that we simply had no choice."

So two longtime legislators in Oregon are stepping down, both with their own failed attempts at bipartisanship. Not every attempt at better politics succeeds. But Bentz isn't done with politics just yet. He's moving up to Congress, a place arguably a lot more partisan than the Oregon Senate.

As for Monnes Anderson, she's put in her time and is ready to be done.

"You know, I'm in my 70s, and I put my heart and soul into being a legislator and campaigning," Monnes Anderson said. "And it was just getting [to be] too much."

"Let us not despair but act. Let us not seek the Republican answer or the Democratic answer, but the right answer. Let us not seek to fix the blame for the past. Let us accept our own responsibility for the future."

**–PRESIDENT JOHN F. KENNEDY, FROM A SPEECH AT LOYOLA COLLEGE ALUMNI BANQUET ON FEB. 18, 1958**

# CHARLIE BAKER

## "LET'S MAKE OUR BRAND OF POLITICS POSITIVE AND OPTIMISTIC."

A Republican in a blue state, Massachusetts Governor Charlie Baker is consistently one of the most popular governors in America. How does he manage that?

In the 2010 governor's race he tried cozying up to the Tea Party. It failed. But sticking to his moderate reputation has worked. It helps that he's liberal on a number of social issues—trans rights, $15 minimum wage, gun safety, supporting the Affordable Care Act, and more.

"I have no trouble being a Republican defined the way I want to define it," Baker said in a *Boston Magazine* story.

It also helps that he's preached against the divisive politics that's so common today.

"Whether it's the grind of the day to day or a crisis, we all need to work together because that's what great public service is all about," Baker said in his second inaugural address. "And in this era of snapchats, tweets, Facebook and Instagram posts, putdowns and smackdowns, I'd ask you all to remember that good public policy is about perseverance and collaboration."

Especially in the era of Donald Trump (whom Baker didn't vote for but has also been careful not to criticize too harshly), politics can be a challenge.

"Politics and public life are not for the faint of heart. It has been and always will be a noisy and cantankerous place," Baker said. "But there is a big difference between open and honest debate on the issues and the sort of character assassination that dominates much of today's dialogue. It is incumbent on those of us in public life to recognize the larger trends that are pulling people apart, and to use our voices to bring them together. It won't end the debate to treat one another with respect, but it could nudge some people who have turned their backs on the whole thing to come back."

"Public life and public service are supposed to be about collaboration and cooperation," Baker said in a 2018 *Boston Globe* opinion piece. "Our founding fathers set up our democracy to be messy and complicated and, by design, wanted people who do not always agree to work together to get things done."

Working together has even extended to his hiring choices.

"I thought to myself, as a lifelong progressive Democrat, OK, he's not going to hire me," Stephanie Pollack told NPR when Baker asked to meet with her. "But it's a great opportunity to tell him what I think he should do on transportation issues."

Baker hired Pollack as his transportation secretary.

"Success is measured by what we accomplish together," Baker said. "People like our collaborative approach to governing. Let others engage in cheap shots and low blows. Let's make our brand of politics positive and optimistic, instead of cruel and dark."

# THREE TEEN CANDIDATES IN KANSAS

## "I MAY NOT BE THE VICTOR, BUT I CAN BE THE INFLUENCER."

Three teenagers who were too young to vote made it on the primary ballot for governor of Kansas in 2018. It was all thanks to a loophole in Kansas law that didn't set an age requirement for serving as governor.

At one point as many as six teenagers were running, though in the end only three made it on the state-wide primary ballots: Democrat Jack Bergeson, Republican Tyler Ruzich, and Republican Joseph Tutera Jr.—all 17 at the time of the primary.

"I wanted to get young people engaged in politics," Bergeson told ABC News. "We've already been successful."

While Bergeson was the first teen in the race, he quickly encouraged Ruzich to join as well. "Go for it," Bergeson told him.

"If I'm [taking] a Democratic message to a young audience and he's out there talking to a young Republican audience, we're going to get more people involved," Bergeson said in a *Christian Science Monitor* interview.

"We need to engage voters of the next generation."

"I may not be the victor," Ruzich said. "But I can be the influencer ... Never let anyone, regardless of your age, tell you your views don't matter."

The teens did have an influence on the election, at least on the Republican side where a hotly contested primary between incumbent Governor Jeff Colyer and Secretary of State Kris Kobach came down to a margin of just 350 votes—about a tenth of a percent. The two teen Republicans, Ruzich and Tutera, may have come in last, but they combined for 3,835 votes—1.2%.

"It's crazy," Tutera said in a *Wichita Eagle* story. "If I hadn't run or Tyler hadn't run, that could have been the difference between who gets elected."

While Koback squeaked by in the primary, Democrat Laura Kelly won the general election in November by five points.

"I feel like even if I get zero votes today, my job will be accomplished because all I'm trying to do is show young people that if I can find haven in the GOP, they can too," Tutera told ABC News.

Months before the primary election, the Kansas Legislature closed the loophole that allowed the teens on the ballot in the first place. In future elections, candidates need to be 18 to serve in state-wide offices and 25 to be governor.

# CORY BOOKER

## "WE NEED A REVIVAL OF CIVIC GRACE."

U.S. Senator Cory Booker from New Jersey famously replied to a mean tweet from Donald Trump by saying, "I love you Donald Trump."

"My mom taught Sunday School and she taught me 'love your neighbor, no exceptions.'" Booker said in a 2019 appearance on *The Late Show With Stephen Colbert*. "Never let someone pull you so low that you hate them."

Loving Trump doesn't mean supporting him, as Booker quickly clarified that he doesn't want Trump as president. But political disagreement should never devolve to hatred.

"I believe in this election more than ever we need a revival of civic grace in our country," Booker said. "We need a more courageous empathy in this country. What's happening in our politics right now is undermining our ability to get big things done. The forces tearing us apart are stronger than the forces binding us together. I think patriotism means love of country—you can't love your country unless you love your fellow countrymen and women."

That willingness to put differences aside and get things done exists even in the most trying times. In 2020, days after the murder of George Floyd and in the midst of national protests, the Senate considered anti-lynching legislation. It passed the House with only four votes against it, but Senator Rand Paul refused to allow it to come before a vote in the Senate, where it had strong bipartisan support.

As angry as he was, Booker refused to attack Paul during an interview with Stephen Colbert, even when Colbert encouraged it.

"People want an enemy," Booker said on Colbert's show in June 2020. But that's not the way. "We demonize each other as if we are [enemies]. We have more animus often toward each other than our common real foes who are laughing at us."

"You cannot win this country by taking on the tactics of those who try to oppress you," Booker said. "This is a moral test of how well we are going to create that more beloved community, because—I'm sorry—the 58 million people who voted for Donald Trump are not my enemy."

Booker understands that getting things done requires coming together, and it's hard to work with someone whom you've vilified. He's taken flak for sharing a meal with Ted Cruz or hugging the late John McCain after his cancer diagnosis.

"We are so vilifying our fellow Americans that even human contact with each other is considered a betrayal of your tribe," Booker said on *Jimmy Kimmel Live.*

That kind of tribalism is stopping progress.

"We agree on these things, but we're not getting things done," Booker said in a CNBC interview with John Harwood. "I want to unite this country, not by what I'm against. It's about what I'm for and who I'm for."

"This nation has gotten far because of our ability to work together," Booker said. "I love the ideals of rugged individualism and self-reliance, but rugged individualism didn't get us to the moon, it didn't map the human genome, it didn't overcome Jim Crow, it didn't build the national highway system under Eisenhower. These are things we did together, and we got to get back to that as a nation."

Coming together helped accomplish bipartisan criminal justice reform with the passage of the First Step Act, one of the few bipartisan pieces of legislation passed during the Trump administration.

"Sometimes they surprise you," Booker told CBS, talking about a process that included Republicans Mike Lee, Lindsey Graham, and Senior Advisor to the President Jared Kutchner.

"I believe in what we can achieve together, and I want to start expanding people's vision for what's possible in our country again," Booker said. "American history is a perpetual testimony to the achievement of the impossible. We can get anything done we want to, we've proven that, but somehow our dreams have gotten a lot smaller in terms of what we're capable of."

We can accomplish those big dreams, but only if we do it together. Because we have a shared destiny.

"The Declaration of Independence ends with this profound declaration of interdependence," Booker said. "It says at the end, if we're going to make this nation work, we must mutually pledge to each other our lives, our fortunes, and our sacred honor. If you turn on TV or watch our politics, trash talking, Twitter trolling—where's the sacred honor in that? Most Americans, Democrat or Republican, believe that everyone should have access to health care. Most Americans, Democrat or Republican, believe that kids should have great public schools. We have so much common ground and so much common pain, but we've lost a sense of common purpose to seize that common ground and deal with that common pain."

Booker ran for the Democratic nomination for president in 2020, along with more than 20 others, but never got much traction. He dropped out in January before the Iowa caucus. There are plenty of theories for Booker's poor performance, but one reason might be that many Democrats wanted a fight with Trump. The eventual nominee, former Vice President Joe

Biden, promised to "Beat Trump like a drum," while Booker kept talking about love.

"This season of America is not a referendum on [Trump]," Booker said. "This is a referendum on us, on who we are and who we are going to be to each other. Will we be a nation of love? And I'm sorry if that sounds like sentimentality or saccharine—but that word, it's sacrifice, it's service, it's struggle, it's saying what happens to you affects me, that injustice any-where is a threat to justice everywhere."

Whether or not Democratic voters in 2020 were ready for Booker's call to come together and do big things, he'll continue to be a powerful voice for unity and progress.

"If you don't like the climate of this country, if there's too much hate, then generate more love," said Booker. "If there's too much meanness, find ways to be more kind to your fellow Americans—not just the ones who agree with you or pray like you or look like you."

Even in the midst of nationwide protest and a global pandemic.

"Right now, we're struggling," Booker said in 2020. "I'm hoping out of this struggle and out of the hurt in this country grows a new harvest of hope."

"What we need most right now, at this moment, is a kind of patriotic grace—a grace that takes the long view, apprehends the moment we're in, comes up with ways of dealing with it, and eschews the politically cheap and manipulative. That admits affection and respect. That encourages them. That acknowledges that the small things that divide us are not worthy of the moment; that agrees that the things that can be done to ease the stresses we feel as a nation should be encouraged, while those that encourage our cohesion as a nation should be supported."

**—PEGGY NOONAN, POLITICAL COMMENTATOR AND SPEECHWRITER FOR PRESIDENT RONALD REAGAN, FROM HER 2008 BOOK *PATRIOTIC GRACE: WHAT IT IS AND WHY WE NEED IT NOW***

# RUTH BUFFALO

## "I WAS NEVER RAISED TO SEE PARTY LINES."

In the blue wave election of 2018, Ruth Buffalo made headlines for being the first Native American Democrat woman elected to the North Dakota Legislature. She's a member of the Mandan, Hidatsa, and Arikara Nation. In a typically Republican state, Buffalo defeated an eight-term incumbent Republican who was the primary author of a voter ID bill that many saw as disenfranchising Native Americans.

But the framing of a young upstart challenging the racist author of a voter ID bill wasn't exactly accurate.

"It's crazy that it happened that way because I just didn't—I guess I didn't know that, to be honest, that he was the prime author," Buffalo admitted to the *New York Times.* "I didn't know until the day after the election, when a current legislator pointed it out."

That hasn't stopped the attacks or accusations that Buffalo has a radical agenda, often lumping her in with the "The Squad" of Democrats who came to Congress in the same 2018 elections.

"I will continue to stand up against injustice and not be silenced," Buffalo told *Indian Country Today.* "I know they're trying to break me."

She says the social media and critics are just a distraction from the real work. *Indian Country Today* notes that "Buffalo claps back with legislation instead of witty responses via Twitter."

"I'm not a politician, but I believe in wanting to make change for our future generations after seeing things that needed to be fixed in my hometown community at a young age," Buffalo told the *High Plains Reader.* "Find ways to help the greater good, and thread the needle toward justice for everyone."

"When I was deciding whether or not to run, I remember thinking, 'What's it going to take to have things change for my children, and for future generations?'" Buffalo said as the keynote speaker at the 2019 Facing Race Awards in Minnesota.

Just two weeks before the election, the Supreme Court decided not to intervene in that North Dakota voter ID law, a ruling that took many by surprise.

"There are good people in North Dakota that see when injustices are happening," Buffalo told *Newsweek.* "With any negatives you can find the positives—that's the goal. ... People still have hope and are mobilizing for change to continue fighting for good overall policies."

Buffalo hopes she can make the North Dakota

Legislature "less polarized."

"I was never raised to see party lines," she said in the *Huffington Post*. "We're all related, we're all on the same team, we're all human beings."

# G.T. BYNUM

## "DOING THE RIGHT THING IS NOT ALWAYS POPULAR."

Tulsa, Okla., Mayor G.T. Bynum describes himself as "a guy with the raw animal magnetism of a young Orville Redenbacher." He did a TED Talk emphasizing data over partisan politics. Bynum is a nerd.

He rode that nerd wave to election in 2016 by 17 points. But it might not help him in 2020 as he runs for re-election. June has been a terrible month for Bynum with a string of high-profile incidents and mistakes—including protests, police violence, and PR flubs. It culminated in Tulsa hosting President Donald Trump for the first campaign rally in months as Bynum, a Republican, struggled to balance welcoming the president of the United States with pandemic protocols.

Bynum refused to cancel the event and met Trump at the airport, but he didn't attend the rally. Predictably, not everyone was happy.

"The reality is there are people who despise President Trump that are just as mad at me for not trying to prevent him from coming here as there are people [who] are mad that think somehow it wasn't as successful because this mysterious shadow group of protesters that neither the media or a security personnel seem to be able to identify kept people from getting in. The reality is you have extremes on both ends," Bynum said in a KRMG interview. "I think you saw the middle prevail."

While June 2020 may be a month Bynum would like to forget, he's used to people being mad at him. Tulsa is home to the worst race riot in U.S. history, a bombing in 1921 that decimated a successful Black neighborhood. As the city approaches the event's centennial, Bynum has been leading the way to confront the city's past, including authorizing a search for mass graves. Predictably, not everyone was happy (again).

"You are doing this to make white people feel bad," a woman accused Bynum while he was having breakfast with his wife and two kids. The diatribe continued for several minutes while the pancakes and waffles got cold. Bynum listened for a few minutes and then defended his actions before the woman left and his kids looked down at their cold breakfast.

"I said: 'Hey, look at me. Doing the right thing is not always popular,'" Bynum recalled telling his kids in a *Washington Post* story. "'Some people will get mad at you. When you do the right thing, not everybody is there to tell you that you are doing the right thing.'"

As he struggles with unprecedented challenges, it's helpful to go back to his idealistic TED Talk.

"Politicians find it easier to throw the red meat out to the base than to innovate," Bynum said. "The conventional wisdom is that to win an election, you have to dumb it down and play to your constituencies' basest, divisive instincts. And when somebody wins an election like that, they win, that's true, but the rest of us lose."

"Let's agree to set aside our philosophical disagreements and focus on those aspirations that unite us," Bynum said. "Let's grasp the opportunity that is presented by innovation to build better communities for our neighbors. Let's replace a focus on partisan division with a focus on results. That is the path to a better future for us all."

Speaking of results, Tulsa is the first city in Oklahoma to host regular citizenship ceremonies since the pandemic shutdown.

"If you're ever feeling down about the division in our country, I highly recommend attending one of these ceremonies," Bynum wrote in a *Tulsa World* editorial. "When you meet people who have come from all around the world because they view Tulsa and Oklahoma and the United States as a beacon of freedom and opportunity, it just fills you with pride in our country."

# DAN CRENSHAW

## "JUST BE PART OF THE SOLUTION."

The blue wave election of 2018 that gave the Democrats control of the House and ushered in the quartet of vocal new progressives known as "The Squad" also brought in Dan Crenshaw of Texas. The former Navy SEAL wears an eye patch because he lost his eye in Afghanistan. He's the conservative response to Alexandria Ocasio-Cortez—just as media savvy and eager to take to social media to make his case.

Crenshaw came to national prominence the weekend before the 2018 election with an appearance on *Saturday Night Live*. The week before, Pete Davidson made a bad joke about the eye patch, so Crenshaw showed up the next week to accept his apology.

"There's a lot of lessons to learn here, not just that the left and right can still agree on some things, but also this: Americans can forgive one another. We can remember what brings us together," Crenshaw said in a serious moment during the bit.

That *SNL* appearance gave Crenshaw a megaphone to talk about his favorite cause: outrage culture.

"But now what?" Crenshaw wrote in a *Washington*

*Post* op-ed after the show. "Does it suddenly mean that the left and right will get along and live in utopian harmony? Maybe Saturday's show made a tiny step in that direction, but I'm not naive. As a country, we still have a lot of work to do. We need to agree on some basic rules for civil discourse."

It's a good pitch for moving toward better politics. He's right about outrage culture—that being "easily enraged by every tweet" isn't sustainable for society—"it's a society at each other's throats," as he put it during his 2019 Conservative Political Action Conference speech.

But it's not clear if Crenshaw always takes his own advice.

"We need to stop the partisan opportunism and blame-game that has infected our country alongside coronavirus. A global pandemic is no time for reckless partisanship—this virus doesn't recognize political parties," Crenshaw said in the midst of COVID-19, and then in the next sentence he took a swipe at Democrat Nancy Pelosi.

"Yeah, I can be sharp," Crenshaw told the *New York Times*. "I will attack ideas very hard. I am not shy about that one bit. So I don't want people to think that because I had a call for civility that that means I shy away from debate and that I'm agreeable. That's not the case. What is the case is that I will not question who you are as a person."

As a hero among conservatives, Crenshaw can sometimes play it both ways. He calls for a higher civic
discourse, but then slams the left at every opportunity. It's how he handles President Donald Trump,
refusing to get dragged into every attempt to critique
the president: "I support his policy agenda," he said
on *The View*. "I don't have to support every character
flaw that he has."

Nor does Crenshaw feel obligated to speak up: "He's
getting slammed for it in the media, so why do I have
to pile on?" he said in the book *The Ones We've Been
Waiting For*.

Crenshaw may be another divisive character in American politics—conservatives love him and liberals love
to hate him. But he does have moments when he
overcomes the division and can bring people together.
Whether it's the *SNL* appearance or the opinion piece
where Crenshaw talks about America in the aftermath
of George Floyd and recognizing our sins but not being overwhelmed by them:

"We can tell the story of our sins—and we should, for
greater perspective—but we must also recognize that
these sins do not render corrupt the foundational
ideals of America. Our imperfections do not define us.
What does define us is the greatness that America has
generated."

Part of Crenshaw's appeal is that he has the same 'tell it like it is' demeanor as Trump, but unlike the president Crenshaw is reasonable, authentic, and likable.

"You want to learn a new perspective? Well, try losing an eye." Crenshaw said in a graduation speech during COVID-19. "Others have been through harder times than this and they got through it, and you can too."

"Just be part of the solution and not part of the problem," Crenshaw said. "That's the only way."

"Our predecessors understood that the ties that bind America are far stronger than disagreements over any particular policy and far more durable and profound than any party affiliation."

**–SECRETARY OF STATE MADELEINE ALBRIGHT
IN A SPEECH AT WINGATE UNIVERSITY
ON MARCH 25, 1997**

# CARLOS CURBELO:

## "I WANT TO GET SOMETHING DONE."

Former Florida Republican Congressman Carlos Curbelo can tell you the middle ground is shrinking. As a moderate Republican first elected in 2014, he was labeled one of the most vulnerable GOP House members going into the 2018 election. He often clashed with President Donald Trump, even refusing to vote for him: "That is not a political decision. That is a moral decision."

Curbelo joined the bipartisan Problem Solvers Caucus, co-founded the bipartisan Climate Solutions Caucus, and also pushed for compromise on major issues, often bucking the standard GOP positions:

- **Gun safety:** "We've kind of inherited this world of binary choices where we either have to repeal the Second Amendment or have no gun safety regulations whatsoever, and younger generations of Americans don't see the world that way. And I want to represent those people and I want to get something done." (The Hill)

- **Climate change:** "To view climate change through partisan lenses only detracts from efforts to discover practical solutions. This debate should not devolve into a petty competition between Republicans and Democrats." (*Miami Herald*)

- **Immigration:** "What we witnessed today was a minority of Republicans joining every Democrat in the House to double down on a failed, broken, inefficient, unfair, and at times cruel immigration system. They prefer the petty politics of immigration instead of the solutions for immigration." (ABC News)

Curbelo sees millennials pushing for a more productive politics: "I see the change coming, where we leave behind this legacy of the baby boomer generation of the all-or-none approach, the politics of personal destruction, the politics of humiliation," he told Charlotte Alter for the book *The Ones We've Been Waiting For: How a New Generation of Leaders Will Transform America*. "Millennial legislators on both sides of the aisle are the ones who are going to turn the page on this dark chapter of our country's politics."

While the dark chapter has been personal for Curbelo—he received a death threat on Twitter in 2018—he doesn't back down. Curbelo held a press conference with the young man who threatened him and refused to press charges.

"If this country doesn't start healing, it is not going to matter who wins elections," Curbelo said on *Cuomo Prime Time*. "We're all going to lose eventually."

Ultimately, the Florida Republican's effort to find middle ground failed. In 2018 he lost to Democrat Debbie Mucarsel-Powell by less than 1%.

"Tonight is not a night for excuses—it's a night for healing," Curbelo said in his concession speech. "This country, our politics, are in a very bad state. Americans who disagree with one another think of themselves as enemies."

Unfortunately, Curbelo continued to experience that political divide even after he left office. In 2019, Democrats initially invited him to testify at a climate change hearing before disinviting him under pressure from leadership—they feared it could give him a platform to boost a possible re-election bid, should he choose to run (he didn't).

"What it has done is expose, again, the reason why things don't get done here, and why the big issues don't get resolved," Curbelo told The Hill. "Because too many people are focused on their own personal political interest, too many people are focused on getting re-elected, and not enough people are trying to build a consensus."

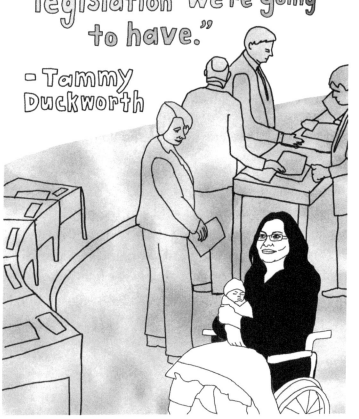

"The more **women** we get into office the more **family-friendly** legislation we're going to have."

- Tammy Duckworth

# TAMMY DUCKWORTH:

## "IT'S NEVER GOING TO BE AS BAD AS GETTING BLOWN UP."

Flying a Black Hawk helicopter in Iraq and surviving a rocket-propelled grenade gives U.S. Senator Tammy Duckworth a sense of perspective about partisan politics.

"It's never going to be as bad as getting blown up," Duckworth said in a 2012 *Chicago Magazine* interview. She lost both legs and some mobility in her right arm, becoming the first female double amputee of the Iraq War.

As bad as political divisions can be, Duckworth knows where her allegiance lies.

"As bad as it's going to be in Washington, I don't owe those people anything," Duckworth said in 2012. "At the end of the day what I owe isn't to Barack Obama, isn't to [then House Speaker John] Boehner, isn't to anyone. It's to the guys who I see once a year to thank them for saving my life. Every year on November 12, we get together, and every year I have to look at these men and say, 'This is what I've done with my life this year; this is what I've done with what you've given me.'"

She refers to November 12—the day a rocket attack took down her helicopter—as Alive Day.

"You can choose to spend the day of your injury in a dark room feeling sorry for yourself or you can choose to get together with the buddies who saved your life," Duckworth told the *Chicago Tribune* in 2006, "and I choose the latter."

While Duckworth strongly supports Democratic issues like the Affordable Care Act and has harshly criticized President Donald Trump, she's also been able to find common ground with folks across the aisle.

Two of her heroes include Republican senators who also served in the military—former Senator and 1996 Republican Presidential Nominee Bob Dole and the late Senator and 2008 Republican Presidential Nominee John McCain.

"If you love this country as much as [John McCain] did, he was willing to sit down and talk with you and work with you," Duckworth said in an NPR interview after McCain's death. "And I love this country more than life itself, and so we found common ground."

Duckworth found more common ground when she became the first senator to give birth in 2018. The Senate unanimously changed the rules to allow senators to bring children under the age of one onto the Senate floor, taking the opportunity to set an example as a welcoming workplace.

"It's about time," Duckworth said as she arrived with her baby to vote.

# MAIA ESPINOZA

## "PEOPLE ARE REALLY LOOKING FOR THAT MESSAGE OF HOPE."

"My community is a lot more blunt than polite, which is refreshing," Washington state activist and teacher Maia Espinoza said during a KUOW interview. "We don't really do 'P.C.'"

As a Republican Latina, Espinoza is used to challenging both sides. In 2018, she ran unsuccessfully for the Washington state House of Representatives. When she realized there was no organization to support conservative Latinos, she started the Center for Latino Leadership.

"I was raised in a conservative household [and] I found Republican candidates tended to align better with my values," Espinoza said in an article in The Lilly. "I'm not happy with what's going on, so I'm doing something about it within my own party."

As a legislative liaison she had to help local Republican lawmakers understand why talking about the "illegals" in a Real ID debate was offensive. But she also gets it from Democrats.

"Yes, white liberals telling me, 'How dare you be a Republican as a Latina.'" Espinoza said. "It reiterates the ignorance of the left toward minority Republicans existing," she told Crosscut.

"Party leaders on both sides need to recognize that nobody belongs to one tribe or the other," Espinoza said. "We can switch teams if we want. And just because we subscribe to one team doesn't mean we agree with everything you stand for. It's actually quite offensive to believe that because you are this stereotype, you have to subscribe to these values or you're some kind of traitor."

A music teacher and entrepreneur, Espinoza is running for Washington's superintendent of public instruction in 2020. She's running because of a state-wide sex education curriculum that passed along a party line vote and is raising eyebrows among some parents.

The debate is getting caustic with current Superintendent Chris Reykdal comparing people opposed to the curriculum to flat-earthers.

"I understand that they want to make sure we're teaching about consent—we appreciate all of that, but [not] the disturbing elements of this," she said in a KIRO story. "We're being referred to as flat-earthers and Holocaust deniers because we're concerned about the content that is being approved."

But Espinoza isn't just on the receiving end. She's also made allegations about Reykdal that prompted a lawsuit over defamation and false statements in a political mailer.

Despite the fireworks, Espinosa advocates a more bipartisan approach.

"I certainly would look at it and have my own task force of parents, with both dissenting people and those who think this is OK—get in a room and take a look at this stuff," she said. "I'm not the type of leader who would come in and say, 'This is my vision and I'm changing it.' I would get people together from both sides, as I do in all my work in politics, to make sure we get something that appeals to everyone."

That work-together approach has roots in her conservative family. As a child she met President Bill Clinton when he was in office. She remembers shaking his hand and then turning to her father and saying, "I thought we didn't like him."

Espinoza's father reprimanded her in front of the president, emphasizing that they must always respect the president, no matter their party.

"What a good lesson," Espinoza reflected in a 2018 KIRO story.

"People are really looking for that message of hope—that there is hope across boundaries, across aisles, and within our own community," said Espinoza. "We can have community and we can be together, even if we disagree politically on some things."

But that doesn't mean everything is kumbaya.

"I do like to liven things up, kick down doors when necessary," Espinoza said with a laugh.

"The increasing polarization that has prompted centrists in both parties to depart has convinced me that the center will hold only if we put the same effort into unity that partisans put into division."

**–U.S. SENATOR SUSAN COLLINS IN AN OP–ED WRITTEN IN 2012**

# BETH FUKUMOTO
## "BUT DO IT WITH KINDNESS."

As the youngest House minority leader in Hawaii, Beth Fukumoto was a rising star in the Republican party. Then she called President Donald Trump a bully and it all came crashing down. The party stripped her of her leadership role and she left the Republican party entirely.

"Speaking out didn't seem like a choice," Fukumoto wrote in her letter resigning from the Republican party. "A call for kindness and respect should have been a nonpartisan message, but it was controversial within the party."

Concerned by Trump's statements during the 2016 presidential campaign—especially his calls to ban Muslims and refusal to denounce the Japanese internment camps—Fukumoto spoke out. Her speech at the 2017 Women's March in Hawaii was the last straw.

"Regardless of who you vote for, kindness and respect should always win," Fukumoto told *TIME* about her speech. "It's our job to make sure that our kids know that bullying's not OK," Fukumoto told NBC.

"What ended up being very problematic for me was that my caucus and others said, 'If you want to stay in leadership, then you need to make a commitment to not criticize the president for the remainder of his term,'" Fukumoto said in The Cut. "And with what we've been seeing in the news with the different executive orders coming out every day, I didn't believe I could make that commitment."

That response was a total shift from why Fukumoto got into politics in the first place. She saw Hawaii being run by an old boys' club that didn't address the real issues.

"I had a ton of hope when I came into the Republican Party," Fukumoto told *Elle* magazine. "In Hawaii, Democrats have a super-majority. It's not good for government when one group has too much power. As a moderate, I believed I could find a place in either party, and I wanted to be an alternative voice for the state. I chose the Republican Party."

Given Hawaii's Democratic control, being part of the minority party meant bipartisanship—a good fit for Fukumoto.

"If you're going to be Republican in Hawaii, it's our role to be constructive partners with the majority," Fukumoto said. "That's how you win as a Republican in Hawaii, by being able to get along with everybody."

But the rise of Trump proved to be too much.

"The party I signed up for was the party that abolished

slavery and broke up the trusts and tried to return power to the people instead of big government or big corporations," Fukumoto said. "We need to start confronting racism and sexism and all these other things, and I don't see Donald Trump taking us down that road."

"I have watched the state of American politics with concern for years. It's becoming increasingly obstructionist, less and less civil," Fukumoto said, noting that both parties have narrowing ideologies. "There are a lot of Democrats who don't want me to be a part of their party because they don't think I'm Democrat enough."

There's a painful irony there, but it's not slowing Fukumoto down.

"This election left Americans afraid of one another, and the tendency is for each of us to stick to our own corners or cling to our labels or just stay out of politics altogether," Fukumoto said in her video resigning from the Republican party. "But now more than ever it's crucial that we start flooding politics with new voices—your voices. ... If you're concerned about the direction of our country, our state or even your town, it's time to speak up, stand up, and work for something better."

Fukumoto is continuing to use her voice as she tries to find her place. In 2018 she ran for Congress but came in a distant fifth in the Democratic primary.

"I'm going to wait to see what the opportunities are," Fukumoto said in *Glamour*. "I think I'm going to maybe run for city council."

Throughout 2020 she's been working to build civic engagement and runs the nonprofit Solving Equal to help women candidates overcome bias and barriers. Whatever she does, she still embodies that central theme of kindness, respect, and getting along.

"Get involved, testify at the legislature, run for office, help on a campaign—but do it with kindness," Fukumoto said in her 2017 Women's March speech. "Show our kids that everyone's voice matters, even when they believe the opposite thing that you do. Teach them that everyone deserves respect and let them know that in the end, love will always win."

# JUSTIN GIBONEY

## "IF WE CAN'T HAVE CONVERSA-TIONS THEN WE CAN'T HAVE A GOOD DEMOCRACY."

Justin Giboney is a bit of an enigma. He's a pro-life Democrat. He's a former football player and a lawyer. He critiques the left and the right, refusing to be pigeonholed. It's no wonder he co-founded the And Campaign, a political organization challenging Christians to eschew party politics and combine biblical values and social justice.

He's not the first to do it.

"In years past, Black leaders, such as Fannie Lou Hamer, fought against conservatives on segregation and against the secular left for the sanctity of life," Giboney said in a *Christianity Today* piece.

Giboney pushes back on both parties. He charges that Democrats "accept the vote of religious voters" but "will treat them as unfit if they try to run for public office." He also challenges Republicans for being pro-life but not "whole life"—"How can you care about the unborn if you don't care about the poor or the immigrant?" he asked the Catholic News Agency.

While Giboney isn't afraid to challenge the major

political parties, he's also quick to accept the blame. After all, he considers himself a Democrat. Working as a lawyer and political strategist in Atlanta, he's managed successful campaigns for elected officials and referendums. He also served as a delegate to the Democratic National Convention in both 2012 and 2016.

"Let's not put all the blame on other people, let's put it on ourselves," Giboney told the *Christian Post* about the 2016 Democratic Party Platform. "The reason the Democrats have gone that way is because we haven't spoken up enough and we haven't been organized enough."

A big part of Giboney's work with the And Campaign is helping Christians engage in the political process.

"The politics of pettiness trivializes even the most serious social and political matters," Giboney wrote for The Hill.

And it's deadly serious. Giboney cites statistics from the 2019 study "Lethal Mass Partisanship" that shows 20% of Democrats and 15% of Republicans said the country would be better if people in the other party just died.

"When we look at statistics that say these people are not fully human, when we look at statistics that say the U.S. would be better if these people were dead, we need to start thinking about where we're going," Giboney says in an online video. "We need to start thinking about Matthew 5:44, 'Love your enemy.' ... Are we taking those lessons and applying them to politics—or do we just apply them in church?"

So how do we get better? It starts by seeing our enemy as our neighbor.

"It's important that we think of our political opponent as our neighbor because it does something about how we see that person at the end of the day," Giboney said in a Detroit Catholic article. "I do think we have to look at people we don't want to talk to and say, 'I take you seriously, I see your dignity,' ... then they come to be your neighbor instead of your enemy."

Then we need to show up and listen.

"Go to local meetings: city council, county commission. Listen to what the issues really are," says Giboney in a *World Magazine* interview. "You can have an impact on the local level a lot quicker than on the federal level, and you can see the changes."

That's how we move from social media showdowns to real conversations.

"If we can't have conversations then we can't have a good democracy," Giboney is quoted as saying on Twitter.

# JENEAN HAMPTON

## "I JUST WANTED TO HELP MAKE KENTUCKY BETTER."

"I'm something you haven't seen: I'm a Black conservative," Republican Jenean Hampton told a crowd in western Kentucky.

In 2015, pundits heralded Hampton as the first African American to win statewide office in Kentucky when voters elected her lieutenant governor alongside running mate Matt Bevin.

"I wasn't running to be first anything," Hampton said in a WDRB interview. "I just wanted to help make Kentucky better."

But when Bevin ran for re-election in 2019, he dumped Hampton at the last hour.

"Maybe a couple of years ago, he started hinting," Hampton said. "But really I didn't find out for sure until 30 minutes before he filed that he was replacing me."

Hampton said she wasn't offended—it was Bevin's prerogative. But she also didn't vote for him. Bevin went on to lose his re-election bid by just over 5,000 votes. The infighting with his own lieutenant governor probably didn't help.

That kind of rejection isn't new for Hampton. Being a Tea Party conservative didn't play well with her Democrat-supporting family.

When her father died in 2014, he "went to his grave mad at me," Hampton told the *Louisville Courier Journal*. "That I'm conservative, Republican, didn't support Obama—he just could not wrap his arms around that."

"I've had conversations with Democrats that I've met and our philosophies are 180 degrees apart," Hampton said. "I've had deeper conversations with them than I was able to have with my dad. He couldn't even put himself in my shoes and at least try to see my perspective about why I believe what I believe, and how it's worked for me."

Initially repelled by Republicans in the Nixon era, President Ronald Reagan's idealism converted her. She felt inspired by NASA and the Constitution.

"A huge part of what formed my opinions was the peer pressure that I got to fail," Hampton said. "These were kids who questioned my good grades, questioned the way I spoke, questioned my choice in music and the fact that I was reading all the time. I just remember wondering, 'Well jeez, when do I get to just be Jenean with my own likes and dislikes.'"

"I just decided that I had more options, and it was up to me to pursue happiness," Hampton said. "I believed that no one owed me money or a job or anything, except the pursuit of life and liberty. ... I believe I'm perfectly capable of running my own life, of making decisions for me."

Sharing her story became one of the hallmarks of Hampton's term as lieutenant governor as she made more than 200 school visits across Kentucky.

"Many teachers recognized the value of students hearing from someone who rose above poverty, bullying, and other adverse conditions," Hampton said in a WBKO interview.

Hampton insists we all have an inspiring story to share: "None of us were overnight successes, and we all experienced speed bumps of some sort. How we handle setbacks often reveals more of our character than our successes."

With her historic run as lieutenant governor behind her, Hampton is open to what's next.

"If I have inspired someone to dream more than they would have otherwise and to maybe reach a little further, then these four years have been so worth it," Hampton said in a WKYT interview. "I hope that they remember that I really came in with a heart to serve and that I actually served."

# CALEB HANNA

## "POLITICS AFFECT EVERYTHING YOU CARE ABOUT."

President Barack Obama inspired many Black children, including a third grader in West Virginia named Caleb Hanna.

"I first got interested in politics in the third grade," Hanna said in a *Charleston Gazette Mail* article. "Here was this charismatic Black man who rose to be president of the United States. I thought, 'I can do that.'"

Hanna is on to an early start. In 2018 he graduated from high school and won election to the West Virginia House of Delegates at the age of 19.

But there is a major difference between Hanna and Obama: Hanna is a Republican. "God, guns, and babies," he said. "That pretty much sums up my political philosophy."

He's supported plenty of solidly Republican positions, like President Donald Trump's border wall. Hanna made national headlines for suggesting West Virginia should contribute $10 million of the state's surplus to the construction cost of the wall.

But he can still surprise. He criticized Trump's choice

of Betsy DeVoss for education secretary and in 2017 congratulated Democrat Doug Jones for his election win to the U.S. Senate.

"We need to stop putting party over people and create a bipartisan agreement on all issues," Hanna tweeted.

Hanna understands he needs to work with Democrats to get something done. That bipartisan streak is refreshing.

"It's the only way to make effective policy," he said in a *New York Times* story. "It's like pulling on a piece of taffy. They pull from one side of the table and you pull on the other side."

Legislating is also a learning process, as Hanna is discovering.

"I definitely want to be a bit more patient," Hanna said in *West Virginia State*, the magazine of the college he attends. "Tensions run high in the chamber there. There's a few times I know you sit there and you listen to everything and you get fired up and I hit my button to speak just to be speaking. Next session I want to try and be a bit more patient."

He's also learning from national politicians.

"I'm not a huge fan of Alexandria Ocasio-Cortez's policies, the way that she goes about things, but I respect

that she is a young person who set out to make a difference. I think you're starting to see that throughout
the country," Hanna said in a *Tennessee Star* article.
"We realize we have to stand up as Americans to do
what's best. That's one thing I ran on in my campaign.
We may be Republicans, and we may be Democrats,
but we're all West Virginians, so we all have to come
together."

And young people are getting involved. Hanna led
a voter registration drive at his high school, getting
100% of eligible students registered to vote.

"You don't have to run for office," he said in a
*Register-Herald* article. "The important thing is to get
registered to vote. Help your favorite candidate.
Politics affect everything you care about."

# JAIME HERRERA BEUTLER

## "IF YOU SPEND ALL YOUR TIME SOWING DISCORD, THAT'S WHAT YOU'RE GOING TO REAP."

At five months pregnant, doctors told Congresswoman Jaime Herrera Beutler that her baby would die. Doctors diagnosed Potter syndrome, a rare condition where the kidneys don't develop. No one had ever survived it.

"That changes your world," Herrera Beutler told The Hill. While doctors pointed to abortion, Herrera Beutler and her husband Dan didn't give up. While staunchly anti-abortion as a politician, that wasn't the deciding factor.

"You're not thinking, 'What's my political stance on this?'" Herrera Beutler told CNN. Instead it was a gut feeling they needed to "contend" for their child. They fought for an experimental therapy and Abigail Beutler was born in July 2013. She needed daily dialysis and a kidney transplant, which came from her father in 2016. Today, Abigail is healthy and happy, often accompanying her mom to Congress.

"Now she's not the only—she's just the first," Herrera Beutler said. "There are other babies who have survived because of her."

With that kind of story, it's no surprise Herrera Beutler has been a champion for mothers. She's the ninth woman to give birth while serving in Congress (and she's done it three times), and she's nursed on the House floor. She co-founded the congressional Maternity Care Caucus, works to reduce maternal mortality, and supports daycare availability—both in Congress and beyond.

"It's shocking to think in 21st century America, we don't have the answers to this," Herrera Beutler said about the challenge of maternal mortality. "What I've found is it's racial, it's regional, it's class, it's gender—there are disparities throughout health care and depending on where you're at, we find the answer, which is why we have to investigate each and every maternal death."

And she's not afraid to do that work across the aisle.

"It is time to make mothers a national priority," she wrote with Democrat Raja Krishnamoorthi in a 2018 editorial.

Herrera Beutler's style is to avoid the spotlight and focus on getting work done.

"I try not to be rude and condescending and provoking," Herrera Beutler said on a town hall call with constituents. "I think that's one way to earn some goodwill on the other side. If you spend all your time sowing discord, that's what you're going to reap."

While Herrera Beutler supports repealing Obamacare and building the border wall, how it gets done is important. She joined Democrats in voting against a GOP health care repeal and for a resolution challenging Trump's emergency declaration at the border. But she also voted against impeachment and called the Democrat-led process a "goat rodeo."

"My goal is not to be [Trump's] foil, but it's not to be his loyal servant," Herrera Beutler told POLITICO. "To the degree that he is serving the people I represent, I'm there, I'm with him. To the degree that there's a problem, I'll oppose him."

But that doesn't stop Democrats from trying to make her guilty by association.

"Wow, I'm the enemy?" Herrera Beutler said. "I didn't even vote for him, for crying out loud."

As a Latina woman, Herrera Beutler is a rare breed in Republican politics—she's the only voting Republican woman of color in Congress right now. The GOP would like her to take a more visible and vocal role in leadership, but she wants to do it on her own terms: "I'm not going to be an attack dog."

"If I'm going to enter into this, I want to have something positive and unifying to bring," Herrera Beutler said. "I don't know if there's a role or not."

# ADAM KINZINGER

## "WHAT CAN WE SOLVE TODAY?"

Republican Congressman Adam Kinzinger is a straight up hero. In 2006, he encountered a knife-wielding man attacking a woman in downtown Milwaukee, and he sprang into action. When talking the man down didn't work, Kinzinger wrestled him to the ground and disarmed him.

"That's what our military teaches officers," Kinzinger said in a *Weekly Standard* article, "how to actually lead in that chaotic situation."

Kinzinger has been an example of leadership, first stepping into public service in college when he ran against a three-term incumbent for a county board position and won. He joined the Air Force in 2003, and still serves in the Air National Guard despite being elected to Congress in 2010.

In 2019, Kinzinger was deployed to the southern border to pilot the RC-26 intelligence, surveillance, and reconnaissance aircraft, where he saw immigration issues firsthand.

"I'm an American before I'm a Republican," Kinzinger said on CNN, explaining why he couldn't support Donald Trump in the 2016 election (but he didn't sup-

port Hillary Clinton either). He's been willing to challenge and criticize his party's president, but he's also
defended Trump, refusing to vote for impeachment.
Kinzinger is the rare politician tired of the partisan
fights.

"I'm willing to give my career to do the right thing,"
Kinzinger told *Esquire*, talking about the real fear
many in Congress have of compromising and inviting a
primary challenge. "I think we need a lot more people
who understand that their actions in Congress have an
impact beyond their re-election."

The extreme partisanship makes it harder to come
together and easier to vilify the other side.

"Nobody in Congress wants to destroy America,"
Kinzinger said. "I think the most ardent, left-wing Democrat wants America to be successful. I want America
to be successful. And the most hardcore right-wing
Republican wants America to be successful. We just
see that process differently, and that's what politics is
for. It's for people that see it differently to somehow
come together and govern."

That kind of perspective makes it easier to be
open-minded, which is part of why Kinzinger changed
his mind on gun safety in 2019. He initially voted
against background checks, but now supports them
and other measures.

"I've gotten to the point where I don't care about the politics—it may hurt me politically, it may help me politically, I don't know. I don't really care," Kinzinger said on TMZ. The more pressing question for Kinzinger is, "What can we agree on? ... What can we solve today?"

"We have nothing to fear but fear itself."

**–PRESIDENT FRANKLIN ROOSEVELT, DURING HIS FIRST INAUGURAL ADDRESS ON MARCH 4, 1933**

# BRENDA KUPCHICK
## "PROGRESS OVER POLITICS."

In 2019, Brenda Kupchick became only the second first selectwoman in the 380-year history of Fairfield, Conn. The Republican leader comes to office in the midst of a politicized scandal and a board of selectmen known for political schism.

"The voters made clear on November 5 that they believe in progress over politics," said Kupchick in the *Fairfield Citizen*. "As we move forward, let us renew our commitment to civility in our political discourse."

That's going to require some heavy lifting after a heated campaign over the ongoing controversy when city officials allowed a company to dump contaminated waste in the city's fill pile, which was then used in projects around town. There are charges of bribery and corruption in the ongoing investigation. Sparks flew, especially online, as the former first selectman tried to defend himself. But Kupchick is ready to turn the page and move forward.

"Tonight, we will start working together," Kupchick said at her swearing-in ceremony. "Instead of talking at each other through social media, we will begin the process of talking to one another face to face. A tweet or a Facebook post should never replace looking someone in the eye."

That's going to start on the three-member selectmen board that has been sharply divided.

"I don't think there's going to be the partisanship that we were seeing in the past," Kupchick said in the *Fairfield Citizen*. "I want us to work together as Fairfielders, and I'm going to really work hard at bringing people together."

"I want to be the first selectwoman of everyone in Fairfield. Not just the Republicans, but the Democrats and unaffiliated," Kupchick said in a Connecticut News 12 story.

In her first year in office, Kupchick worked to modernize how city hall operates and bring in more business, before shifting gears to lead the response to COVID-19. While it's a challenge to juggle all the demands, Kupchick is committed to moving Fairfield past the status quo.

"I didn't run for any office just to be a professional politician," Kupchick said in a Westfair article. "I have a four-year term, and if at the end of it the voters decide they don't want me, I'll go home, pay more attention to our business and have a normal life."

"But I want to get some real work done here," she added. "If you can't do that in a meaningful way, why are you even in public service?"

Whether it's overcoming scandal or working through a pandemic, Kupchick recognizes the value of bringing people together.

"We are Fairfield, we together make up the town of Fairfield, and we should all be working together because this is our town, right? This is our town." she said.

"[Republicans and Democrats both] said to me, 'We just want to put our swords down and work together,'" Kupchick said in the *Fairfield Citizen*. "I hope that's my legacy."

# CASSANDRA LEVESQUE
## "WE ARE UNSTOPPABLE."

When 17-year-old Girl Scout Cassandra Levesque learned that girls as young as 13 could get married in her home state of New Hampshire, she thought, "OK, I need to change this," according to a *New York Times* story.

She did her research, met with representatives, and pushed for legislation.

But then Levesque got pushback from Republican Representative David Bates who said, "We're asking the legislature to repeal a law that's been on the books for over a century, that's been working without difficulty, on the basis of a request from a minor doing a Girl Scout project."

That didn't faze Levesque.

"I wanted to tell him that I'm more than just a little girl selling cookies around his neighborhood," she wrote in a Girl Scout profile. "I'm a Girl Scout, and Girl Scouts are the leaders of today. We are future presidents. We are lawmakers—the majority of female senators and members of the House of Representatives are Girl Scout alums."

So Levesque ran for office herself. It took some

convincing and she had to make a pro/con list. But she ran and she won at the age of 19.

"We, the future generations, are no longer going to sit idly by and watch as our nation loses its humanity," she wrote on Twitter in the aftermath of the 2018 election. "We will rise up and not only demand change, we will lead the charge to be the change!"

Of course serving as a legislator is still a lot of work, especially in New Hampshire where it's basically a volunteer job (legislators get a $100 salary plus mileage reimbursement). While Levesque's push to raise the marriage age failed in 2017, the New Hampshire Legislature did raise it to 16 in 2018. She's still fighting to raise it to 18 and feels better equipped as a legislator.

"I felt very nervous because I didn't know anybody, but I know the people on the committee, I have relationships with other legislators," Levesque said in *The Concord Monitor*. "Now, I'm confident in what I know, I have facts. I have a six-inch binder just full of data."

Sometimes doing the work and finding the facts isn't enough. Politicians still need to come together.

"For the most part we try to be bipartisan as much as we can," she said at a Duke University event. "We try to make sure that we get things done."

Especially on a divisive issue like gun safety, Levesque sees the need for politicians to get along.

"We have to work together to find a way to come together on this issue," Levesque said in a *Barrington Town News* interview. "Standing on separate sides and yelling back and forth is not making any progress."

While some try to make an issue of her age, Levesque sees it as a strength.

"A lot of us, for years, we've just sat and let people silence us, and so finally we're sick of it and we're standing up," Levesque said in a *Boston Globe* story. "We want to get our voices heard and make a difference."

"At Girl Scouts, we change laws. We change the world," she said. "We are unstoppable, and we won't be ignored."

"All great change in America begins at the dinner table. So, tomorrow night in the kitchen I hope the talking begins. And children, if your parents haven't been teaching you what it means to be an American, let 'em know and nail 'em on it. That would be a very American thing to do."

**–PRESIDENT RONALD REAGAN DURING HIS FAREWELL ADDRESS ON JAN. 11, 1989**

# JEFF LUNDE

## "WE'RE SO DIVERSE WE HAVE A REPUBLICAN MAYOR."

"We consider ourselves the world's largest Liberian city outside of Liberia. We are the most diverse large city in the state of Minnesota," said Brooklyn Park, Minn., Mayor Jeff Lunde in a profile on mayors making a difference by The Hill. "We're so diverse we have a Republican mayor."

Liberians make up about 9% of Brooklyn Park, so Lunde was eager to work with Democrats to support a pathway to citizenship for Liberians. Many Liberians sought refuge after a civil war in the 1990s and were facing deportation with the end of their temporary protected status. Democrats and Republicans worked together to pass the measure, and President Donald Trump signed it into law.

"This past year we worked closely with our federal delegation to come up with a solution and not once did politics get in between doing the right thing for our residents," Lunde said in a press release from Representative Dean Phillips, a Democrat.

Phillips invited Lunde to attend the State of the Union as his guest.

"[I tell people I] believe in unicorns," Lunde said in a *Sun Post* story. "We proved that something can get done."

Lunde is unapologetic about working across the aisle. Elected as mayor in 2011, Lunde ran for state Senate in 2016. But when GOP candidates disparaged Muslims, Lunde spoke out.

"I don't know a single Muslim leader who wants to give aid and comfort to a terrorist. But I've heard about a young girl being picked on because she wears a hijab," Lunde said in a *Star Tribune* article. "This isn't how we do business."

Lunde organized a forum of local faith leaders, with two dozen priests, ministers, and imams attending, to show solidarity in the face of the attacks.

"As the largest ... diverse city in Minnesota we feel an obligation to lead," Lunde said. "The national dialogue, the rhetoric on both sides drives me absolutely crazy. That's not how we do things in Brooklyn Park. We actually talk and listen."

But it doesn't always go smoothly. Despite doing more for immigrants than previous mayors, Lunde is still criticized for not doing enough. In 2017, the city passed a resolution supporting refugees and immigrants in response to the Trump administration's travel bans. Lunde said he fielded hundreds of calls and messages from concerned residents and attended 41 community gatherings with various groups in response to the issue. Lunde recommended tabling the resolution as the council debated various changes, though six weeks later they ultimately passed the original resolution without watering it down.

Lunde lost that state Senate campaign in 2016, but he continues to lead in Brooklyn Park, running for and winning a third term in 2018.

"Our job is not to get involved in food fights. Our job is to make sure people have food to eat," Lunde told The Hill in 2020. "People just want a better life, and I think we welcome them here."

"We are not enemies, but friends. We must not be enemies. Though passion may have strained it must not break our bonds of affection. The mystic chords of memory, stretching from every battlefield and patriot grave to every living heart and hearthstone all over this broad land, will yet swell the chorus of the Union, when again touched, as surely they will be, by the better angels of our nature."

**–PRESIDENT ABRAHAM LINCOLN IN HIS FIRST INAUGURAL ADDRESS ON MARCH 4, 1861**

"If we are serious about healing our democracy there is no substitute for talking with our neighbors and not just our friends."

- Matt Little

# MATT LITTLE

## "WE WILL NEVER HEAL OUR DEMOCRACY HIDING BEHIND A KEYBOARD."

Matt Little is a state senator in Minnesota who believes in the power of door knocking. In a Feb. 18, 2020 opinion piece in the *Star Tribune,* Little argued that "door knocking is the heart and soul of a successful political campaign and a healthy democracy."

The fresh-faced Senator comes to the job with a sense of humor, a self-effacing style, and a heavy focus on the practical. But that doesn't mean he shies away from a fight. His door-knocking editorial came in response to another piece that questioned the efficiency of the common political practice.

"We will never heal our democracy hiding behind a keyboard or polished ad," Little wrote. "We must shake someone's hand. Look them in the eye. Tell them what we believe and work through that conversation."

Little knows a thing or two about what works. He became the youngest mayor of Lakeville, Minn., at the age of 27 in 2012. In 2016, he took a big step up to state senator, knocking on a lot of doors and talking to a lot of voters.

During his term, Little started a Senate Committee on Banned Bills to hear popular but politically difficult bills that weren't getting a hearing—proposals like background checks for gun purchases, paid family leave, restoring the right to vote for former felons, and a constitutional amendment for gender equality.

They're the kind of issues that have broad, bipartisan support. The kind of issues you learn about when you talk to real people.

"If we are serious about healing our democracy, there is no substitute for talking with our neighbors and not just our friends," Little wrote in his opinion piece. "It can't be done with TV ads, mass mailings, and slick social media that push us apart and keep us anonymous. Those uncomfortable conversations, standing with the screen door propped open, are more than just effective campaign strategy, they are the heart and soul of a healthy democracy."

And Little welcomes those conversations, whether they happen on a front porch or at a restaurant table.

In 2018, after a rash of protests against Trump officials at public restaurants, Little tweeted that the public can talk to him anytime. It's part of being an elected official.

"If I'm out in public eating lunch or having dinner, you have every right to come up to me and tell me what you think," Little said. "That's how public service works."

Little is also quick to embrace the video-based social media app TikTok. With more than 140,000 followers, he's easily the most popular politician on the controversial site. His authentic style is a good fit as he jokes and lip syncs, while also making the occasional policy point.

"I think people have enjoyed the positivity, the humor, the relief from the typically divisive nastiness that politics comes with," Little told POLITICO.

That positive and encouraging attitude shines through for Little. While things have changed a bit in 2020 and door knocking isn't a great fit with the pandemic, he still finds a way to connect.

"Maybe you're tired and burnt out on politics. The hyper-negativity has you despondent. That's OK. It happens," Little tweeted. "You can take a step back. Take a breather. But you can't give up. Focus on the good you see. Focus on the progress, however small it may seem. You've got this."

"Don't wait for someone else to come along and fight for your community—do it yourself."

**—SECRETARY OF STATE, U.S. SENATOR, AND TWO-TIME PRESIDENTIAL CANDIDATE HILLARY CLINTON IN THE FOREWORD TO THE 2017 BOOK *RUN FOR SOMETHING: A REAL-TALK GUIDE TO FIXING THE SYSTEM YOURSELF***

# *LISA MURKOWSKI*

## *"CONSENSUS SHOULD NOT BE A DIRTY WORD."*

In 2002, Lisa Murkowski became the first senator from Alaska who was actually born in Alaska. She is the state's sixth senator, which reminds you just how young the state of Alaska is, officially becoming a state in 1959 (born in 1957, Murkowski was actually born in the Territory of Alaska).

That's a good reminder that Alaska is a little different from the Lower 48.

"I don't think most Alaskans fit neatly into the Republican box or the Democratic box," Murkowski told the *Press Herald*. "They don't think of themselves that way."

That might be why Murkowski connects. In 2010 she lost her primary to a Tea Party challenger, but she stormed back with a write-in campaign, becoming only the second U.S. senator in history to win as a write-in.

"I don't fit neatly into anybody's political boxes," she said, "and I think that sometimes disturbs people."

In 2016, she won on the Republican ticket, but the runner up was a Libertarian. The Democrat finished a distant fourth, behind an Independent.

Politics are also a little different in Alaska. Conservative for sure, but there's also an odd pairing of environmentalism and energy, as well as union support. Despite being a Republican, Murkowski is solidly pro-choice.

"Over half the people in this state chose not to align themselves with any party at all," Murkowski told *TIME*.

That's given Murkowski a pragmatic streak that often puts her at odds with her own party.

"I am not one of those who wants Obama to fail," she told Katie Couric in 2010. "If he does well, that means the country's doing well. We don't have time as a nation to spend all of what we do blocking."

In 2010, Murkowski talked about her differences with the Tea Party, emphasizing her willingness to have conversations with Democrats in negotiations over earmarks.

"I think we have got to be willing to put everything out on the table," Murkowski said in a Real Clear Politics interview. "If we can't get beyond all of the sacred cows that we all have out there, we're never going to get to tackling these very difficult decisions."

In 2013, she talked about having breakfast with Democrats to talk energy policy.

"If we can advance things that are smaller but still make a difference, I'm OK with that," she told the *Washington Post.* "Even in this very polarized partisan world you can advance legislation. I have to believe that, or I wouldn't want to get up every morning."

"I am willing to listen, I am willing to sit down with colleagues on the other side of the aisle to see if we can't develop good policies from good ideas that come from different perspectives," Murkowski told the *Anchorage Daily News.*

In 2018, she became the only Republican senator to vote against the confirmation of Supreme Court Justice Brett Kavanaugh. (In doing so, she actually voted 'present' in a procedural move that allowed her Republican colleague to attend his daughter's wedding. "It will not change the outcome of the vote," Murkowski told NBC. "But I do hope that it reminds us that we can take very small, very small steps to be gracious with one another. And maybe those small, gracious steps can lead to more.")

Those moderate moves have sparked a backlash from President Donald Trump. Though often a critic of Trump, Murkowski voted against impeachment. But when General James Mattis released a scathing criticism of Trump's response to nationwide protests in 2020, Murkowski described General Mattis' statement as "true and honest and necessary and overdue." Trump responded with a harsh tweet threatening to endorse anyone with a pulse against Murkowski in 2022.

"Consensus should not be a dirty word in the political process," Murkowski said in a Real Clear Politics interview in 2010. "And yet there are some who believe we should never be reaching across the aisle. I couldn't disagree more."

"I've definitely experienced things from many perspectives and I think that's helped bridge the divide."

-Svante Myrick

# SVANTE MYRICK

## "I COULD DORK OUT OVER SIDEWALK LEGISLATION."

Here's all you need to know about Svante Myrick, the youngest and first Black mayor of Ithaca, N.Y.: He turned his reserved parking space into the city's smallest park where he can connect with residents, complete with a suggestion box.

"People aren't used to having unfettered access to public officials," Myrick said in a Governing.com story. "But unfettered access is kind of what my generation is all about."

Myrick first ran for mayor in 2011 and became the city's youngest mayor at 24. Ithaca voters re-elected Myrick for a third term in 2019. His political journey started in 2007 when he gave up an internship in Barack Obama's Senate office in order to run for Ithaca's Common Council.

"I was like, 'What would Obama do?'" Myrick said in the book *The Ones We've Been Waiting For*. "I think Obama would run for city council." So he did. And he won.

Myrick discovered Obama after the famous 2004 speech at the Democratic National Convention. His grandmother sent him Obama's memoir and he read it cover to cover, disappointed that someone like Obama—someone very much like Myrick—couldn't be president.

"I assumed that if you're born with a name like Barack Hussein Obama, or you're raised by a single mother, there's a ceiling on your success," Myrick said in an interview with the Cornell alumni magazine. "He showed me there's no ceiling. The only limit to what you can accomplish is your own imagination. He definitely changed my life."

Born into homelessness and raised in poverty, Myrick has struggled. But he also graduated from an Ivy league school.

"I lived a life of paradoxes," Myrick said. "I've definitely experienced things from many perspectives, and I think that's helped bridge the divides."

Leading Ithaca forward has forced Myrick to do more than bridge divides. He inherited a $3 million deficit and still had to tackle ambitious projects. His administration tackled affordable housing, police reform (before George Floyd), and a massive infrastructure project that had been kicked down the road by his predecessors.

"I think the decision to do it was a youthful one," Myrick told *TIME* in a story about millennial leaders.

"Because I was naive about how easy it would be, and because I was like, 'What's two years of pain if we can get this right for a hundred years?'"

Much of Myrick's success is because he's fascinated by the policy details. He's a dork.

"A dork is somebody who cares about stuff that nobody else cares about," Myrick said in a Visit Ithaca interview. "I care about sidewalk policy, you know? So I could dork out over sidewalk legislation for a good chunk of time."

But he's also deeply connected to Ithaca, in a way you might not expect from someone who first ran for office while in college. Here's how he described his first run for mayor:

"I've never felt anything like it. I quit my job three months before the election. I was working at Cornell and I spent 14 hours a day just knocking on people's doors. Stranger's doors. And fending off their dogs and playing with their kids and just talking to them about what brought them to Ithaca, and what they cared about, and what they wanted to see done. And I knocked on every door in the city three times. And by the end of it I felt like a spider in a web. I just never felt so immersed in a place. I felt like I was an actual part of that place, the same way your arm is a part of your body. I mean, I knew what the people on Wood Street were worried about and were thinking about, and I knew what the people on Madison were worried about and thinking about, which is two different parts of town. But I knew also what they had in common. And that feeling of community connection, that feeling of knowing your neighbors, I mean it's the closest thing to familial love. That sort of love you feel in a family unit. But at a scale of 30,000. I mean, I've never felt that way before. I think the last two weeks of my campaign were... yeah, the best moments of my life."

"We are Americans first, Americans last, Americans always. Let us argue our differences. But remember we are not enemies, but comrades in a war against a real enemy, and take courage from the knowledge that our military superiority is matched only by the superiority of our ideals, and our unconquerable love for them."

**—U.S. SENATOR AND TWO-TIME PRESIDENTIAL CANDIDATE JOHN MCCAIN DURING HIS SPEECH AT THE 2004 REPUBLICAN NATIONAL CONVENTION**

# COLLIN PETERSON

## "WE'VE WASTED MONEY ON STUPIDER THINGS."

"Bipartisanship gets things done," Representative Collin Peterson of Minnesota said on Twitter. That could be his mantra. First elected in 1990, the longtime Congressman is consistently noted as one of the most bipartisan legislators.

"My job in Congress is to work with whomever I can to improve peoples' lives," Peterson told the *Fergus Falls Journal.* "No one can do that by always voting the party line."

It's a lot easier to be bipartisan when you disagree with your party on a lot of issues. And Peterson does. As a Democrat, he voted against the Affordable Care Act, he's pro-life, and he's proud of his A rating from the NRA.

"If I hear the words 'common-sense gun legislation' one more time, I'll throw up," Peterson said in a *Star Tribune* article. "This is poll-tested nonsense."

In many ways, Peterson is a throwback. He's one of the old school Blue Dog Democrats, a group of moderates who often compromised with Republicans. But they're a rare breed these days.

"There aren't many like me left in Congress," Peterson told MPR. "Rural Democrats are few and far between and I'm concerned that rural America is getting left behind."

That's where Peterson has made his mark. His deep roots in farming have convinced many to cross party lines. Peterson's district went for Trump by 31 points in 2016, though Peterson beat his Republican challenger by five points. Peterson himself didn't even vote for Hillary Clinton.

While Peterson says he didn't vote for Trump either, he was one of only three Democrats in the House to vote against impeachment.

"How can it be that after all the testimony, every Democrat thinks the president has committed an impeachable offense and every Republican thinks he has not?" Peterson said in a statement about his vote. "Throughout my career, I have worked from the guiding belief that only through bipartisan action can we address the country's most pressing challenges."

That's been Peterson's guiding star—bringing people together across party lines to get things done. Even when it upsets his own party. During the government shutdown of 2019, Peterson urged Democrats to compromise and give Trump money for the border wall with strings attached. He felt his comments were misconstrued.

"Anybody that sticks their head up gets it shot off," Peterson told MinnPost. "The furor caused yesterday—people didn't look at what I said, and this is the problem. The press has allowed it to become polarized."

"In the old days, the Blue Dogs would have been all over this," Peterson lamented as his bipartisan efforts weren't gaining traction. "People say, [the wall] is a waste of money. Maybe it is... We've wasted money on stupider things than this. Maybe it isn't going to do much good, it's probably not going to do much harm. Why are we getting wrapped all around the axle on this?"

Even if it's not popular, Peterson sees bipartisanship as the only way to get things done.

"Every issue we work on should be bipartisan," Peterson said in an interview with the National Grain and Feed Association. "The issues we work on impact too many people to get caught up in partisan fighting. But it can't just be lip-service. For too long, people have talked about bipartisanship as meaning the other side agrees to their ideas. That's not how it's going to work here. Folks are going to need to realize both sides may leave unhappy, but with a workable legislative product. That's a win in my book."

Leaving both sides unhappy? It's no wonder the National Republican Congressional Committee calls him "Cranky Collin."

While Republicans are eager to unseat Peterson—and they may have their best shot at it in 2020—he says they're "dreaming" if they think he'll retire. He'll likely be the last Democrat to hold this very red district.

Peterson laughed off concerns that a late retirement announcement might make it hard for a Democrat to run: "I don't think anybody could win that district," he told POLITICO. True to his roots, Peterson decided to run again in 2020 so he could usher another farm bill through Congress.

# *JARED POLIS*

## *"WE ARE BETTER TOGETHER."*

In 2018, Colorado elected the first openly gay governor in the United States, Jared Polis.

"I must begin by saying I'm very conscious of the fact that there were many brave people over the years who made it possible for someone like me to be standing here giving a speech like this," Polis said in his inaugural speech. "I am grateful and forever indebted to those who came before me—who struggled for equal rights, who stepped up for public service in all forms, who made difficult sacrifices and worked faithfully toward a brighter future for our state, our nation, and our world."

Polis is also an amateur poet.

When U.S. Senator Ted Cruz read *Green Eggs and Ham* by Dr. Seuss in a filibuster attempt to defund Obamacare in 2013, Polis responded with a poem of his own: "No, I do not like Ted Cruz reading *Green Eggs and Ham*, and shutting down government without giving a damn."

Despite his partisan political poke at Cruz, Polis generally works to find common ground.

"Our nation is experiencing a period of growing

divisiveness and rising tribalism," Polis said during his inauguration. "We reject that brand of politics."

In 2009, Polis emailed supporters a poem lamenting the partisan divide: "While in Washington the Pachyderms and asses did battle / Fighting and bickering and sounding like rattlers / Hissing and striking, hemming and hawing, / Displaying plumage and pomp / Never listening always talking."

"We are a diverse country, but we are one country," Polis said in a 2012 speech at the Democratic National Convention. "And we are at our best when we come together as Americans, not despite our differences, but in celebration of them."

Part of the challenge is not politicians, but the partisan supporters.

"What you have is this institutional Hatfield and McCoy sentiment coming from our constituents, where the base of both sides doesn't want people to get along," Polis said on Fox News. "Too often, we hear from our base, 'Don't talk to the other side, don't work with them.' And even though I feel that most Americans don't feel that way, they want the parties working together, those folks don't call in. Those folks don't have marches, right? ... What needs to happen is the majority of the Americans in the middle, they need to start calling in and saying, we want you guys to work together, because that is what will change the result."

Even when politicians want it, bipartisanship isn't always smooth sailing. Polis wanted across-the-board income tax cuts, but his own party—with a majority—didn't. Polis vetoed five bills in his first year, often due to implementation issues or unintended consequences. Polis also refused to support sanctuary state laws that would protect immigrants from Immigration and Customs Enforcement (ICE), preferring local control—a move that angered other Democrats.

Nevertheless, nearly 95% of bills Polis signed in 2019 were bipartisan.

"The notion that we're all in this together is a much better approach to solving problems than trying to go it alone," Polis said in his 2020 State of the State speech. "When we realize that our fates are connected and that we are better together, we can solve any problem we encounter."

"What can we do, all of us together to try to make our politics better. And I speak to both sides on this, because all of you know it could be better. And all of you would feel prouder of the work you do if it were better. ... We should insist on a higher form of political discourse that is based on respect."

**—PRESIDENT BARACK OBAMA, DURING REMARKS AT THE ILLINOIS GENERAL ASSEMBLY ON FEB. 10, 2016**

# QASIM RASHID

## "THE BIGGER RISK IS FOR ME TO STAY SILENT."

Qasim Rashid is running a long-shot campaign for Congress. A Muslim activist, author, and attorney, he ran for Virginia Senate in 2019 and lost by 15 points. In 2020 he's running for Virginia's 1st Congressional seat in a district that's strongly Republican. The 2018 Democrat challenger lost by 11 points, and previous races were 20- and 30-point blowouts.

But even a long-shot political campaign can still make a difference.

As a Muslim and Pakistani immigrant, Rashid deals with a lot of negativity: "Just some of the most grotesque things that you could ever say to anybody," Rashid told CBS News.

How we respond to that kind of hate can make all the difference.

When Oz Dillon flung anti-Muslim and hate-filled tweets at Rashid, something Dillon has done to many liberal politicians, Rashid responded with something different.

"My faith instead teaches me to serve all humanity,"

Rashid tweeted. "So I've donated $55 to his GoFund-Me to help him and his family cover crushing medical debt."

Rashid encouraged his followers to donate as well, and they did, helping Dillon pay off more than $20,000 of debt.

"I stared at the screen just reading it over and over and over," Dillon said. "He reached across that gap and took my hand."

Dillon asked Rashid for forgiveness and the two met, discussing issues and dispelling misconceptions over coffee. Dillon still made it clear he wasn't going to vote for Rashid, but he did ask Rashid for a yard sign "so everyone can see it."

"You know, that's not what it's all about," Rashid said. "The first thing I said to him was, 'I'm not doing this for any favor.'"

While Rashid might not have won Dillon's vote, he did make a friend.

"He has showed me that there is good in all walks of life," Dillon told NBC News.

It doesn't always end that well. Rashid reached out to another person who sent hateful messages and donated to his GoFundMe.

"He was gleeful that, you know, I had helped him. He

was clear that he still maintained his racist views," Rashid told PRI. "So, maybe I'm naive, maybe I'm just a hopeless fool."

Still, Rashid sees these attacks as opportunities.

"I think the bigger risk is for me to stay silent and not try to neutralize this hatred," Rashid said. "Because if I do that, as my children get older, they'll have to suffer through it."

# REGINA ROMERO

## "WHOEVER YOU VOTED FOR—
## LET'S WORK TOGETHER!"

In 2019, Tucson elected former City Council member Regina Romero as their first female mayor and first Latino mayor since 1876.

"I am humbled and honored to be your mayor," Romero said during her inauguration. "Never in my wildest dreams that I would have imagined the daughter of an immigrant farmworkers would be here today starting an historic journey with you as your mayor."

But one of the curiosities is that a Latina mayor in a blue city in a red state took an interesting stance on a sanctuary city measure that was on the ballot in 2019. The measure sought to make Tucson the only sanctuary city in Arizona, protecting undocumented immigrants from federal enforcement. Romero opposed the measure.

"I have supported ordinances to protect immigrants, with or without papers; people know where my heart is," Romero told Telemundo. "As it is written, the proposal has many holes and would not protect us from budget cuts."

Romero's argument is that the Republican-controlled

state legislature will come down hard on Tucson if they become a sanctuary city. There have been threats to cut off funding, and Romero fears that ultimately more people will be harmed than helped.

"No amount of electoral success is worth the division that will be sown throughout our communities if this initiative makes the ballot," Romero said in a KGUN article.

As much as she wants to avoid the wider conflict, Romero is also frustrated by the lack of local control.

"What we have seen, in the last 12 to 15 years, is that the state of Arizona has tried to micromanage Tucson," Romero told *Phoenix* magazine. She'd like to see the state legislature empower "more cities and towns throughout the state to be self-governing—which I think is actually a very conservative thought, in principle."

She's also frustrated with the proponents of the sanctuary city measure.

"I wish we would have been able to have a discussion with those people that wrote the sanctuary city initiative because 60% of what the initiative calls for we're already doing in the city of Tucson," Romero said in an AZPM story.

Romero wants to bring everyone to the table and find a solution together.

"I want to continue working for the betterment of every single one of our residents, including our undocumented residents of Tucson," Romero said in another AZPM article. "If all of the stakeholders sit together … and write ordinances and laws in the city of Tucson that can continue advancing that agenda, I think that is the best way to go about it."

The sanctuary city measure ultimately failed, with 71% of voters opposed to it.

"When you want to get stuff done, it's a really good idea to sit down and try to hash it out," Romero said in a Tucson.com article.

During the primary, Romero took heat when it was revealed that her campaign co-chair had donated thousands of dollars to President Donald Trump's campaign. The co-chair, Cody Ritchie, had also donated to previous Republican presidential candidates.

"Cody Ritchie is a Republican," Romero explained in a Tucson.com story. "We disagree on almost everything, but what we do agree on is that we both want to see the quality of life in Tucson better for the betterment of our citizens. We both want to see a good, clean city, good roads, and good parks."

Working together can not only draw criticism, but it's often a slow process: "Change is a long-term career," Romero said. One of her early initiatives will take a while to bear fruit—combating rising heat in Tucson by planting one million trees.

But Romero is all about pushing her city forward, even when it's hard.

"We must constantly challenge ourselves in ways that, at times, may make us feel uncomfortable," Romero said in a KGUN story during the racial unrest following the killing of George Floyd. "We can always do better: in the policies we set as mayor and council, in our police department, and as fellow Tucsonans. If we are 'comfortable' with where we're at, we are doing something wrong."

It all comes back to her rallying cry for Tucson: "We are one. Somos Uno."

"At a time when our national politics have been sown with division, Tucsonans remain united by our shared desire to promote a safe, just, and sustainable city that provides economic opportunity for our families and future generations," Romero said during her inauguration. "This movement is open to everyone—whatever your background, whatever your party, whoever you voted for—let's work together! We will always be one Tucson—somos uno."

# MAX ROSE

## "WE GET SHIT DONE."

You're not likely to find a less polished member of Congress than Max Rose. He describes himself as "eminently hateable." He proudly notes in his Twitter bio that the *Washington Post* calls him a "human terrier." When POLITICO asked about his campaign in April 2020 at the height of COVID-19, he responded, "I don't give a fuck about politics right now." His supporters wave signs that say, "Max Rose gets s#!@ done." You're supposed to wear a tie in Congress, and when asked why he doesn't, Rose retorts, "Why don't you wear a fuckin' tie?"

If he's a little rough around the edges, it's only because he's focused on getting things done.

First elected to Congress in 2018 at the age of 33, Rose is a veteran of Afghanistan. An IED destroyed his armored Stryker vehicle, nearly killing him. He was awarded the Purple Heart—and came away with an important lesson about the value of government. He tells the story on the campaign trail that a two-star general came up to him in the hospital and told him five years ago he would have died.

"After far too many soldiers died, Congress finally got their act together," Rose said in a POLITICO story.

"They put the right people in a room, they gave them resources, they put partisanship aside, and they said, 'Solve the damn problem!' That used to be the story of this country. I am only alive today because that's what Congress is actually capable of."

That's his story in a nutshell—put the bickering aside and get big things done.

"I want to see the Interstate Highway Act of this generation," Rose said in the book *The Ones We've Been Waiting For,* arguing for big bipartisan ideas over progressive party politics. "The Apollo project for battery technology."

Rose said the COVID-19 pandemic is a perfect example of what the federal government can accomplish, but we're squandering it.

"No one but the federal government could storm the beaches of Normandy... No one but the federal government could send a man to the moon... No one but the federal government could win the Cold War," Rose said in a POLITICO interview. "We are in exactly the same situation. No one but the federal government can get this done."

All the things needed during a pandemic—testing, hospital beds, PPE, "those are not inevitable," Rose said. "But they're possible with government leadership. And we've got to get it done."

Rose could care less who gets the credit—even if that ensures a re-election victory for President Donald Trump, a president for whom Rose voted to impeach, risking his own re-election.

"Nothing would make me happier, nothing, than to see this president utilize all the tools at his disposal to win this war as the commander in chief that he is, and to own that success," Rose said. "And if that success means that we beat COVID-19 and he wins re-election, then so be it. God bless him. ... But I have not seen his administration assert its authority in the ways that it could."

"When I put on the uniform, we didn't fight for blue or red states—we defended the United States," Rose said on Twitter in response to Trump's comments about blue state bailouts during a pandemic. "Let's do our jobs, stop the games, and save lives."

Rose backs up his talk with action. He's still in the National Guard and was called up during the pandemic to help put up hospitals in New York—weeks after him and his wife adopted a new baby.

"I have confidence that as Ronald Regan once said, 'If we, for a moment, don't worry about who takes credit, we can get unbelievable things done.'" Rose said in an SILive.com story. "I am motivated deeply by the desire to show people that government can work, that government doesn't have to be a problem, that it can be a positive service."

Rose is a rough-around-the-edges, Blue Dog Democrat in a very red district. But he's not interested in party politics, he's interested in getting things done.

"When you do what's right, not what's just best for your party, we get shit done," Rose told SILive.com.

"Ask not what your country can do for you, but what you can do for your country."

**–PRESIDENT JOHN F. KENNEDY, DURING HIS INAUGURAL ADDRESS ON JAN. 20, 1961**

# BEN SASSE

## "START FROM THE ASSUMPTION THAT OUR OPPONENTS ARE LIKE US."

"Can anyone believe this bozo is a U.S. senator?" reads Nebraska Senator Ben Sasse, reading mean tweets about himself from supporters of President Donald Trump in a clip reminiscent of late night TV.

Though he rode a Tea Party wave to the U.S. Senate in 2014, Sasse did not support Trump in the 2016 election and became one of his few Republican critics to still seek re-election.

Sasse is used to being a little unconventional. He's been known to drive for Uber and has handed out sandwiches at a Nebraska football game.

"I like to work alongside and for Nebraskans," Sasse explained on Twitter.

Maybe it's because Sasse hasn't been a lifelong politician or maybe it's because he maintains that connection with everyday people, but Sasse is a vocal critic of Congress.

"Right now most people in Washington, their biggest long-term thought is about their own incumbency,"

Sasse said on *The Late Show With Stephen Colbert*. "They don't want to ever leave that place and so they don't want to do hard stuff."

"You know, things are bad, right?" Sasse said on NPR. "I mean, there's data that shows 20, 25 years ago, about 14% of Americans thought the other political party was evil. Today, it's about 40%."

"But it seems like lawmakers have a hand in this, right?" reporter Audie Cornish asks Sasse on NPR. "If there are red and blue jerseys, you guys are handing them out."

"Absolutely," Sasse responds, owning his part of the blame.

"I think it's also important for us to recognize that what we're struggling with right now didn't start two years ago. This isn't about Donald Trump," Sasse said in 2018. "And no other politician can fix it either. This is not a two-year-old problem. This is a two-plus-decades problem in the making."

Sasse blames both parties for contributing to the problem, and he's thought about leaving the Republican party many times.

"I conceive of myself as an independent conservative who caucuses with the Republicans," Sasse said on *State of the Union With Jake Tapper*. "Frankly neither of these parties have a long-term vision for the future of the country."

But the reality is that it's deeper than the Democrats or Republicans.

"If our 2016 presidential election was the most lurid and dismaying election of our lifetime—and it was, without a doubt, a five-alarm dumpster fire—it was still only the consequence of deeper problems, not their cause," Sasse writes in his 2018 book *Them: Why We Hate Each Other and How to Heal.*

"Liberals and conservatives no longer believe the same things," Sasse writes. "We don't understand how our opponents believe what they believe, and we soothe our lonely souls with the balm of contempt."

Did you catch that diagnosis? Ultimately Sasse sees the root of all this bipartisan rancor as a result of the technological revolution and our resulting loneliness.

"We're hyperconnected, and we're disconnected," he writes. The book champions being rooted in local community—family, friends, meaningful work, and faith (whether that's religion or more philosophical).

"What is needed is for people from both sides to agree that political and policy divides are not our primary identities or our primary divides," Sasse writes. "As Americans, we need to agree first on the universal dignity of all people, before we descend to the more divisive but less important debates about the prudential use of the levers of government power."

If you want better politics, Sasse argues, we need to be better people. That starts with knowing our neighbors, forming deeper friendships, and getting along with people. When we start with a foundation of friendship, it's a lot harder to be divided by political disagreements.

"Start from the assumption that our opponents are like us—decent folks who want what's best but who start from a different place," Sasse writes.

# HILLARY SCHIEVE

## "DON'T TELL ME WE CAN'T FIND SOMETHING IN COMMON."

In 2014, Hillary Schieve ran for mayor of Reno, Nevada, as a nonpartisan. She won.

"It's definitely not common, but it helped me stand out for sure," Schieve told *Elle* magazine. "People felt like I wasn't a politician; I didn't have an agenda. I made decisions that I thought would be best for people, and that resonated."

Schieve is fiscally conservative and socially liberal, and she found that people saw different things in her campaign.

"There's no Democratic or Republican way to clean a street," Schieve said. "I wish we could all see that we don't fit into these little boxes. Let's be honest. I know a lot of Republican women that are pro-choice. I know a lot of Democrats who are small business owners and want less regulation."

"There's so much divisiveness on both sides; it's nice not to have to choose," Schieve said. "Everyone likes the taste of beer, right?" she told POLITICO. "So don't tell me we can't find something in common."

Schieve's foray into politics started with bureaucratic red tape. When the city wanted to charge her business $5,000 to move a sign, she decided to do something.

"I said to myself, 'I'm not going to complain. If I want to change it, I need to run for office.'" Schieve said. She started by winning a city council seat in 2012.

"When government is open to collaboration, innovation can happen much more quickly," Schieve said in a *Common Edge* story.

Now that she's part of government, Schieve does her best to make collaboration and innovation a reality.

"I've learned to listen really well," Schieve said in a TEDx speech. "A lot of listening is really important because people have really great ideas and sometimes government does not do well with innovation or forward thinking or things like that."

Schieve also says that gratitude and compassion are an important part of the work. Schieve saw a figure skating career disappear with an illness that nearly killed her and led to a kidney transplant. The experience taught her to be thankful.

"It makes you connect better with others, and I think it's important really to honestly have a lot of compassion in your life," she said.

That kind of grounding allows her to stay focused and overcome the criticism.

"I'm really proud of the work, but it isn't easy. You need a really thick skin," Schieve said. "I always tell people I never knew how fat and stupid I was until I logged on Facebook. It's an incredible tool, but social media can be damaging. Luckily, I know how to stay focused."

Schieve has focused on revitalizing Reno—bringing in new business, lowering the unemployment rate, and adding affordable housing.

"I do believe that we can come together, as people, to make the world better," Schieve said. "I believe that with my heart of hearts. No matter our differences, we have common goals."

# PAT SPEARMAN

## "EQUALITY IS BREAKING OUT ALL OVER THE WORLD."

In 2017, Nevada became the first state to pass the Equal Rights Amendment (ERA) in 40 years, thanks in part to the work of Nevada State Senator Pat Spearman. Originally passed by Congress in 1972, the ERA fell short of the 38 states required to ratify it in order to become a Constitutional Amendment. The ERA sought to give men and women equal rights, something critics have argued is unnecessary and symbolic.

"It's a very powerful symbol," Spearman responded to that criticism, comparing it to other symbols like the Pledge of Allegiance or a wedding ring.

The ratification of the ERA faces major challenges considering the original 1979 deadline.

"There's no shelf life for equality," Spearman told the Huffington Post.

Spearman understands the long fight for equality. As a Black, gay woman serving closeted in the Army for 29 years and then as a pastor, she's seen discrimination of all kinds.

"There's not any part of me that I can bring to the

conversation that has not experienced discrimination," Spearman said. "As a woman I've experienced discrimination. Discrimination in life. Discrimination in the military. Discrimination, even in church."

Spearman faced sexual harassment in the military that she says hindered her career. Likewise, her LGBTQ status would have ended her career.

"Galatians 6:9 says, 'Be not weary in well doing, you will reap the harvest if you do not faint,'" Spearman said. "We got tired, but we did not faint. We became weary, but we did not faint. We were vilified, ostracized and criticized, but we did not faint. I encourage my colleagues to support and pass this legislation. We persist, in the name of all that is good."

"We're not talking about special rights here, we're talking about equal rights." Spearman said. "Equality is breaking out all over the world. You can slow it down, but you can't stop it."

In 2019, the Nevada Legislature became the first majority female legislature in the nation. That female representation meant the passage of a number of bills important to women, tackling issues including sex trafficking, sexual misconduct, equal pay, and child marriage.

"The idea of having a female majority has left a sense of pride that I can't even explain to you," Spearman told CBS News. "The women who are here this time, doesn't matter which party, when we're passionate about something we just push for it."

"I've been tired so long, now I am sick and tired of being sick and tired, and we want a change."

**—CIVIL RIGHTS ACTIVIST FANNIE LOU HAMER IN A SPEECH IN NEW YORK ON DEC. 20, 1964**

# ELISE STEFANIK

## "IF YOU'RE WILLING TO LEAD, PEOPLE WILL SUPPORT YOU."

In 2014, Elise Stefanik became the youngest woman ever elected to Congress. At the age of 30, the Republican had already worked in the George W. Bush administration and for vice presidential candidate Paul Ryan.

"As someone who's frequently been the only woman and the youngest person in the room this past year, I believe it's really important to bring other young women to the table," Stefanik told *TIME*.

In 2018, Stefanik handed the youngest mantle to 29-year-old Democrat Alexandria Ocasio-Cortez. When Stefanik was first elected, the previous youngest woman offered her advice, and so Stefanik passed it on and gave Ocasio-Cortez some tips.

"Success means that you serve as a role model for a next generation of women who believe they can run and win at a young age," Stefanik wrote in a *USA Today* piece. She noted that many of these young women have reached out to her. "Encourage every single one of these young girls and women, regardless of partisanship."

That non-partisan spirit would certainly be tested. While Stefanik has criticized President Donald Trump's rhetoric and voted against his Tax Cuts and Jobs Act of 2017, she also made headlines defending him during the impeachment process and pushing back on Democrats. She was also one of only eight Republicans to support the Equality Act, a 2019 bill that would add LGBTQ protections to the Civil Rights Act.

Stefanik has also bucked her party by specifically supporting women through her Elevate PAC—even in primaries, something Republican leadership has discouraged. When National Republican Congressional Committee Chairman Tom Emmer said getting involved in primaries was a mistake, Stefanik tweeted, "I wasn't asking for permission."

"Women bring a unique perspective," Stefanik said in a *City & State* article. "I think having more at the table makes us more effective policymakers."

Ironically, Stefanik clashed with Ocasio-Cortez over this very issue after the 2019 State of the Union. The two traded barbs, but ultimately Stefanik tweeted, "We need to work to elevate women's voices across the aisle."

Doing the work is a theme for Stefanik. Her advice to Ocasio-Cortez recalled turning down an interview from Fox News' Chris Wallace immediately after her first election, but accepting it in her second term.

Wallace asked why and Stefanik explained: "I told him it was because I first wanted to deliver wins and results and earn the respect of my colleagues."

"The life lesson is that if you're willing to lead, people will support you," Stefanik said.

"We are capable of even greater heights if we return our awareness and actions back to an era of civility." -Erin Stewart

# ERIN STEWART

## "WE CAN DISAGREE WITHOUT BEING DISAGREEABLE."

In 2013, New Britain, Conn., elected 26-year-old Erin Stewart as the youngest mayor in history. In 2019 she won re-election to a fourth term.

The Republican inherited a $19 million deficit that she closed in her first term. Stewart brought in a new tech center, launched the largest solar project in the city's history, and brought in $12 million in state and federal grants for streetscape improvements, all while keeping unions and city workers happy. In 2019 she earned an endorsement from the American Federation of State, County, and Municipal Employees (AFSCME), a union that has never endorsed a Republican mayor in New Britain.

"We appreciate the deep respect Erin has shown for city employees and the vital services they provide," AFSCME Executive Director Jody Barr said in a *Hartford Courant* article. "Her willingness to work collaboratively to solve problems and meet challenges transcends politics or personalities."

Stewart has also brought that savvy millennial approach to the job, hosting Facebook Live events before City Council meetings to update residents and answer questions.

Her videos get hundreds of comments and thousands of views, "But we can't get two people to show up at city hall," Stewart told *TIME*. "That's fine, I'll bring government to you."

Something that isn't new is the negativity she faces as mayor—especially a female mayor. A study shows that 68% of mayors report being demeaned on social media and 49% report harassment. Women in the study were twice as likely to experience psychological abuse or violence.

"Now we're body shaming?" Stewart asked in frustration after a demeaning Facebook comment appeared from a former state Democratic leader, according to a *Hartford Courant* article. "What happened to 'Love wins?' That's what we're working for in my city."

More insults came from a Democrat running for City Council during the 2019 campaign (he ultimately lost a 14-person race for five at-large seats), prompting Stewart to address the negativity in her inauguration speech.

"I don't know about all of you, but I'm tired of it—the divisiveness, the negativity, the name calling," Stewart said according to the *Hartford Courant*. "We are capable of even greater heights if we return our awareness and actions back to an era of civility."

Stewart was also quick to accept blame herself: "While I believe myself to be an eternal optimist, I know that I can be as guilty of this as anyone," she said. "I can only control my own actions—so this pledge starts with me."

"We can disagree without being disagreeable," Stewart said according to the *New Britain Herald*. "So let's set an example for the state, and quite frankly, the entire nation, by treating each other with respect and maintain civility in our discourse."

"When you see something that is not right, you must say something. You must do something. Democracy is not a state. It is an act, and each generation must do its part to help build what we called the Beloved Community, a nation and world society at peace with itself."

**—CIVIL RIGHTS LEADER AND CONGRESSMAN JOHN LEWIS, WRITTEN SHORTLY BEFORE HIS DEATH AND PUBLISHED IN THE *NEW YORK TIMES* ON THE DAY OF HIS FUNERAL, JULY 30, 2020**

# WHAT'S NEXT

So where do we go from here?

In 2016, I watched the election with seething range, alternating between wanting to know every tidbit of breaking news and blocking it all out. The outcome seemed obvious to me, so I didn't get involved—like a lot of people.

Predictably, I had a lot of regrets. So I spent the next several years getting involved in local politics. I attended my first City Council meeting. I called my representatives in Congress. I knocked my first door for a political campaign.

I wasn't going to sit back again and be disappointed in 2018. To be clear, 2018 certainly had a few disappointments—one of the candidates I door knocked for lost her primary—but I didn't have any regrets the day after the election.

I'm writing this book in the lead up to the 2020 election. In my limited experience of the past few years, I've learned a few things about getting involved. If we want politics to be better, we have to do something about it. You can't just sit back and complain (well, you can, but don't expect anything to change).

If we want things to change, it's incumbent on us to be a part of making that change happen.

I believe our democracy is better when people are involved and engaged. The constant battle is driving people away, and our country is lesser for it.

And if I've learned anything else, it's that political change is mind-numbingly slow. Don't expect to knock on a few doors or make a few phone calls and see change start to happen. I started pushing for a bike and pedestrian underpass in my town in 2017. It seemed like an "easy win" we could actually accomplish locally. As I write this book in the summer of 2020, they still haven't broken ground on that underpass—but they've awarded the bid, and everything is lined up for it to happen. Turns out this underpass project started back in 2012, if not earlier.

Progress is slow. You need to keep your expectations in check.

But the only way we can make any progress at all is by digging in and doing the work.

Here are three things I recommend to start taking action and creating better politics:

## 1. TIME TO LEARN

The first thing you should do is educate yourself. There's a lot going on in the world and it's easy to be clueless about politics. So start paying attention and learning a few things.

# WHO REPRESENTS YOU?

A good place to begin is finding out who represents you in all levels of government. Start at the top and work your way down:

- President:

- Senator 1:

- Senator 2:

- U.S. Representative:

- State Senator:

- State Representative:

- County Commissioner:

- School Board:

- Mayor:

- City Council:

Depending on where you live, these might not all apply. Or maybe there's another level to consider (I'm not even listing judges). The point is to do your research.

And don't overlook any position. The people in power at the bottom of that list actually have a lot more control over your day-to-day life than the people at the top of the list. In many cases, you can actually talk to the people at the bottom of the list and get real and honest responses (you might get that near the top too, but you're more likely to get a formulaic response).

# LOOK AT THE ISSUES

Once you learn who these people are, start paying attention to the issues. See what's going on in your community and do some research. When you've sorted out what's happening, go back to who represents you. What do they say about these issues?

But more than their stance on the issues, pay attention to how they conduct themselves. Are they mean and dismissive? Tell them that's not OK. Are they polite and considerate? Give them a high-five. (Seriously: Elected officials are much more likely to hear from angry constituents, so positive feedback goes a long way.)

Advocating for issues is an important way to be involved in the political process. But that's not going to lead to better politics by itself. Instead of trying to win on any specific issue, learn to see these politicians as people. Maybe they embody better politics and maybe they don't. But you can be a part of encouraging them to be better.

And if that doesn't work, maybe you should run to replace them.

# 2. STOP FIGHTING

Everybody likes a good fight. Whether it's the playground or the political arena, we all gather around to watch the show, egging on the participants.

But going along with that sort of display isn't going to lead to better politics. Instead we need to lead by example and walk away from the fights.

I know, it's easier said than done.

While writing this, a friend posted a dumb political meme to Facebook and I took the bait and commented. I did have the sense to delete my rage-filled attack and stick with the facts about how the meme was misleading. But then it descended into link swapping, as if one good article would win the argument.

So instead of punching back with an even smarter article, I took a breath. I moved away from the meme and the rabbit trail of arguments that wouldn't get us anywhere. Going back to the main issue, I asked if we could agree on some basic things surrounding that issue. Maybe we can find some common ground and maybe we can't, but there's more potential to have a productive conversation than if we keep slugging it out over a silly meme.

It's hard, but try taking these steps to avoid the fight:

1. Step back from the fight and try to see your opponent as a person. Especially on social media it's too easy to dive into an argument with little regard for anybody.

2. Look for common ground. Has anybody ever been persuaded by a Facebook thread? It may end friendships, but it rarely changes minds. So instead of fueling the fight, find something you can agree on.

3. Think before you post. It's also helpful to think about the other end of social media. Are you posting something that's going to start a fight? Social media can be amazing, but it's also the worst. Use it for good.

4. Have real conversations. Instead of always arguing, have real, in-person conversations where the goal isn't to win but to get to know somebody. Ask people what they think (like my grandma does) and listen. (If you already agree, avoid the 'isn't the other side dumb' conversation and go deeper.)

In the heat of the 2016 election, Michele Obama famously said, "When they go low, we go high."

And everybody promptly ignored her advice and waded into the 2016 fight.

If we want better politics, we have to take the high road. We have to ignore the memes, walk away from useless arguments, and be better. That means not taking the petty shot. That means ignoring a social media thread. That means it's OK to disagree. It's not like whoever comments last wins.

That doesn't mean we should never fight. Sometimes there are issues where you need to stand your ground. But the key is to go high. Make your point, but do it with grace. Don't just dunk on a flimsy argument.

## 3. DO YOUR PART

More than having a voice in politics, if we want politics to be better, we really need to push for that change. Politicians are incentivized, often with gobs of money from donors, to keep up the partisan punching. So advocating for better politics—asking politicians to be nicer and lead instead of divide—is a tall order.

Anything we can do to champion improvement is going to be a win.

Look for ways to make the political process better. Often our system falls into backstabbing and bickering because it's designed that way. Congressional seats are gerrymandered so one side wins and another loses, but the people are the real losers. In the long run, fighting those kinds of injustices helps people regardless of party. Whether it's fair election maps, more voting options, or even a change like ranked-choice voting that could move us away from our current two-party gridlock are all ways to make politics better.

Look for things everyone can agree on. Push for transparency. Fight for government that works.

If everyone who grew frustrated by divided politics got engaged instead of throwing their hands up, we could make some real change.

You can be part of that solution. Maybe you should run for office. We need people who will look for common ground, not another win for their side. There are a lot of folks who should run who would never think they should run. So think about it.

OK, running for office isn't for everybody. But you can help someone who would champion better politics run and win. Your support in their campaign could make the difference in an election. How many times do we hear about contests that are decided by a few votes? You never know: Your efforts to door knock could make those few votes worth of difference.

## LET'S GET TO WORK

If we want better politics, we have to do something about it.

So educate yourself. Talk to your representatives and tell them you're tired of partisan bickering.

Lead by example and stop the political pouting. Instead of posting yet another political meme, have a conversation with someone who disagrees with you.

Do your part by supporting issues that level the playing field and make better politics possible.

# ABOUT THE AUTHOR

**Kevin D. Hendricks** lives in West St. Paul, Minn., with his wife and two kids. He runs his own freelance writing and editing company, Monkey Outta Nowhere. He's been blogging since 1998, has written several books, and runs the hyper-local news site West St. Paul Reader.

Learn more at KevinDHendricks.com.

# ABOUT THE ILLUSTRATOR

**Carolyn Swiszcz** lives in West St. Paul, Minn., with her husband and daughter. Primarily a painter-printmaker, she also makes illustrations and publishes a zine, *Zebra Cat Zebra*.

Learn more at CarolynSwiszcz.com.

# ACKNOWLEDGMENTS

Nobody reads acknowledgments, right? That's OK, I've got a bunch of people to thank and this is where we put all the secrets.

## Politics of Joy

I don't know where exactly this project started, but I'm going to blame it on Erin Murphy, a former state representative in Minnesota, and her #PoliticsOfJoy campaign for Minnesota governor in 2018. You may notice that Erin Murphy is not Minnesota's governor. She lost in the primary. But I supported her: I wore the T-shirt, marched in the parades, knocked on the doors.

I met her during a training for door knocking. She told me she learned how to campaign by talking to people. She said if you listen more than you talk, you're doing it right.

Murphy had an energy to her campaign that I found infectious. It's why I got involved. That #PoliticsOfJoy thing wasn't just a hashtag. It was real.

Even though she lost, the fire her campaign generated stuck with me. I want to see a politics that's defined not by fighting and opposition, but joy and hope.

That sounds sappy and idealistic, but I don't care. I'll pick hope over hate every time.

So thank you to Erin Murphy, her running mate Erin Maye-Quade, and the whole campaign.

## Get Local: West St. Paul

It's also impossible to write a book about politics and not acknowledge West St. Paul. I live in this first-ring suburb of 20,000 people in the Twin Cities and it's where I first got involved. I've attended council meetings, rallied for causes, supported candidates—I even launched a hyper-local news site, West St. Paul Reader.

We got strangely involved in local politics in West St. Paul and witnessed an uprising after an incident of sexism against West St. Paul's first female mayor, Jenny Halverson. So I'm greatly indebted to the many people in West St. Paul who have inspired me, argued with me, volunteered with me, and helped wrestle our little suburb forward.

## Kickstarter Support

Thanks to our Kickstarter backers who literally made this project happen: Erik Anderson, Stacey Bartron, Jack Becker, Andy Berndt, Edward Bordas, Robert Carnes, Sheila Cina, Jon Cline, Anthony Coppedge, Ben Cotton, John Deen, Justin Deering, Matt Ehresman, Jonathan Ehrlich, Ellie, Lisa Eng-Sarne, Michael Fallon, Anne Frewin, Liz Gillen, Marcus Goodyear, Mike Hadley, Kelley Hartnett, Andy Havens, Susan

Heil, Kerry D. Hendricks, Pam Hendricks, Dr. Sanjiv and Namita Jain, Morgan Kavanaugh, Jeremy Keillor, Kiki, Joe and Holly Kimbell, Rich Kirkpatrick, Kirsten, Ed Kohler, Adam Legg, Shelley Leiphart, William Leung, Darlene Lewis, The Libbus Family, Bill Lindeke, Jon Lipp, Lyford Family, Chad Manbeck, Jeffrey Martin, Darcy McKenzie, Jennifer McNally, Arioch Morning-star, Ian Mwangi, Ellen A. Onderko, Andrew Olson, Joe Porter, Rachel Quick, The Schempp family, Tim Schraeder, Rev. Meiko Seymour, Lindsay Steinbauer, Matt Storlie, Jenny Wine, and Jeanette Yates.

And a bunch of you who opted not to have your names listed in the book. You know who you are. Thanks. Ultimately 119 people came together to make this book a reality. Thank you.

I bugged more than 600 friends on social media and email, begging them to check out this project and support it. I probably burned whatever social capital I've built up over the years, and I did it in the midst of a pandemic when no one was eager to spend money. Thanks to everybody who responded, and thanks still to the people who appreciated the idea but couldn't support it at the time. And thanks to everyone who didn't unfriend me.

**Making It Happen**

Early on in this project I pitched the idea to several people to see if I was crazy. Some saw early drafts and some just listened to me rant. Thank you for encouraging me to keep going: Brad Abare, Adam Bottiglia, Robert Carnes, Robyn Gulley, Kelley Hartnett, Morgan Kavanaugh, Adam Legg, Cory Miller, and Kelsey Shuster.

Thanks to Jack Becker for pushing me to see this as more than a project I did by myself and something I can invite others into. I don't know what that means yet and where this will go, but I appreciate the push.

I didn't have the time, money, or connections to personally interview everyone in this book, so this project relied entirely on secondary sources. Lots of scouring Google. This book wouldn't exist without the incredible journalism from professionals who do the work. In a time when journalists face constant attack, we need them more than ever. Thanks for your work.

I've published a lot of books and do a lot of writing, but you really don't want me doing the design. So I'm grateful to Darci Read for lending her design skills to make everything look better. I thought we'd just get her for the cover, but she foolishly agreed to do the interior design as well (saving my sanity).

Finally, this project wouldn't be nearly as fun, inviting, and engaging without the illustration of Carolyn Swiszcz. Her gentle prodding and pushing has made this project way better than it otherwise would have been. She turned me into an illustration and spawned a ridiculous video and made this whole thing a lot of fun. It's been a long ride and a lot of work, but I'm so grateful. You should really check out Carolyn's work. She has a fun zine called *Zebra Cat Zebra* that's the most wonderful surprise when it shows up in your mailbox. Do yourself a favor and subscribe.

**Best for Last**

Thank you to my family for putting up with me while working on this project. Book projects can be all-consuming, so I appreciate the grace. Thanks to my wife Abby for listening to all my ideas and not being too harsh when they're silly. Thanks to Lexi and Milo for door knocking with me in 2018. Your anger that things are dumb is inspiring and humbling. We should have done a better job making this world a better place for you.

But it's not too late. You can do it yourself, Mayor Milo. And Lexi, one of these days the girls will get their shot and run the world (Also, thanks for being my over-paid researcher).

Finally, thanks Grandma. Who are you voting for? (And sorry for the profanity in the Max Rose chapter.)

# NOTES

**Introduction**:

**video Kinzinger made about conspiracy theories and COVID-19:** Adam Kinzinger, "Unplug the Rage Machine to Combat the Spread of Misinformation," May 20, 2020, http://youtube.com/watch?v=c-i8Fvo7NRo

***The Today Show***: Simon Vozick-Levinson, *RollingStone*, "Bono: I've Grown Very Fond' of George W. Bush," November 30, 2018, https://www.rollingstone.com/music/music-news/bono-george-w-bush-world-aids-day-761747/

**N.J. Akbar:**

**WKYC:** Danielle Wiggins, WKYC, "Akron man turns challenges into triumphs, becomes Vice President of Akron Board of Education," January 16, 2020, https://www.wkyc.com/article/life/akron-man-turns-challenges-into-triumphs-becomes-vice-president-of-akron-board-of-education/95-d415edbf-56a6-4e8c-ae17-360d188b369d

**Medium piece:** Ohio Democratic Party, Medium, "Highlighting Black LGBTQ+ leaders in the Buckeye State," June 30, 2020, https://medium.com/@ohdems/highlighting-black-lgbtq-leaders-in-the-buckeye-state-46a0d18145ba

***Beacon Journal***: Katie Byard, *Beacon Journal*, "Kent State assistant dean N.J. Akbar enjoys helping students achieve dreams and find success," August 15, 2015, https://www.beaconjournal.com/article/20150815/news/308159526

**virtual commencement speech:** N.J. Akbar, "2020 Firestone Commencement Speech," May 25, 2020, https://www.youtube.com/watch?v=jVFyp44lkms

**Justin Amash:**

**speech from the House floor:** Juliegrace Brufke, The Hill, "Amash says it's Congress's duty to impeach Trump," December 18, 2019, https://thehill.com/homenews/house/475189-amash-says-its-congress-duty-to-impeach-trump

***Washington Post***: Justin Amash, *Washington Post*, "Justin Amash: Our politics is in a partisan death spiral. That's why I'm leaving the GOP," July 4, 2019, https://www.washingtonpost.com/opinions/justin-amash-our-politics-is-in-a-partisan-death-spiral-thats-why-im-leaving-the-gop/2019/07/04/afbe0480-9e3d-11e9-b27f-ed2942f73d70_story.html

**CNN**: Haley Byrd, CNN, "Justin Amash announces presidential exploratory committee," April 28, 2020, https://www.cnn.com/2020/04/28/politics/justin-amash-exploratory-committee/index.html

**The Hill**: Marty Johnson, The Hill, "Amash says he's happy not feeling 'bound to a particular party'," October 11, 2010, https://thehill.com/homenews/house/465441-amash-says-hes-happy-not-feeling-bound-to-a-particular-party

**RollingStone**: Andy Kroll, *RollingStone*, "Rep. Justin Amash: 'Most Members of Congress Don't Think Anymore'," January 20, 2020, https://www.rollingstone.com/politics/politics-features/justin-amash-iran-impeachment-congress-937760/

**Twitter:** Justin Amash, Twitter, June 30, 2020, https://twitter.com/justinamash/status/1278076496603688964

**he tweeted:** Justin Amash, Twitter, July 6, 2020, https://twitter.com/justinamash/status/1280179422553952260

**Twitter:** Justin Amash, Twitter, May 18, 2019, https://twitter.com/justinamash/status/1129831627872493574

**Free Thoughts podcast**: Justin Amash, Free Thoughts, "Who Broke Congress?" June 12, 2020, https://www.libertarianism.org/podcasts/free-thoughts/who-broke-congress-rep-justin-amash?hss_channel=tw-354990034

**Newsweek**: Jason Lemon, *Newsweek*, "Justin Amash Argues Republicans and Democrats Are 'Destroying Our System,' Says They Are 'Making It Impossible' to Enjoy Our Lives," May 3, 2020, https://www.newsweek.com/justin-amash-argues-republicans-democrats-are-destroying-our-system-says-they-are-making-it-1501668

**Bushra Amiwala:**

**Glamour**: Bushra Amiwala, *Glamour*, "I'm a Muslim Woman Who Ran For Office, but People Were More Focused on My Identity Than My Politics," June 4, 2018, https://www.glamour.com/story/running-for-office-as-a-muslim-woman-people-were-more-focused-on-my-identity-than-my-politics

**14East**: Dylan Van Sickle, *14East*, "Meet Bushra Amiwala: The DePaul Junior Newly Elected to the Skokie School Board," April 5, 2019, http://fourteeneastmag.com/index.php/2019/04/05/meet-bushra-amiwala-the-depaul-junior-newly-elected-to-the-skokie-school-board/

**Brown Political Review:** Neil Seghal, Brown Political Review, "BPR Interviews: Bushra Amiwala on Embracing Tech and Rejecting PACs," July 20, 2020, https://brownpoliticalreview.org/2020/07/bpr-interviews-bushra-amiwala-on-embracing-tech-and-rejecting-pacs/

**Seventeen**: Bushra Amiwala, *Seventeen*, "I'm a College Sophomore and I'm Running For Office," March 16, 2018, https://www.seventeen.com/life/a19458975/bushra-amiwala-college-sophmore-running-for-office/

### Two Retiring Senators in Oregon

**Mail Tribune:** Claire Withycombe, Jake Thomas, and Sam Stites, *Mail Tribune,* "Key Oregon legislators to call it quits," December 12, 2019, https://mailtribune.com/news/state-news/key-oregon-legislators-to-call-it-quits

**Argus Observer**: Leslie Thompson and Nik Streng, *Argus Observer,* "Republican lawmakers walk out over carbon bill," June 20, 2019, https://www.argusobserver.com/news/republican-lawmakers-walk-out-over-carbon-bill/article_a34e54d8-939e-11e9-ad94-b39107fa5c1e.html

**Walkouts aren't unique:** whmacken2013, *Thinking Oregon,* "'Legislative Walkouts Are Undemocratic.' Nonsense." February 29, 2020, https://thinkingoregon.org/2020/02/29/legislative-walkouts-are-undemocratic-nonsense/

**Abraham Lincoln:** Dave Umhoefer, Politifact, "Wisconsin Senate Minority Leader Mark Miller says Abe Lincoln jumped out of a window to deny a quorum," May 30, 2011, https://www.politifact.com/factchecks/2011/may/30/mark-miller/wisconsin-senate-minority-leader-mark-miller-says-/

### Charlie Baker

**Boston Magazine**: Alyssa Vaughn, *Boston Magazine,* "Charlie Baker Still Refuses to Take a Stance on Impeachment," December 20, 2019, https://www.bostonmagazine.com/news/2019/12/20/charlie-baker-trump-impeachment/

**second inaugural address:** Charlie Baker, WBUR, "Transcript: Gov. Baker's Inaugural Address For His 2nd Term," January 3, 2019, https://www.wbur.org/news/2019/01/03/transcript-charlie-baker-second-inaugural

**Boston Globe:** Charlie Baker, *Boston Globe,* "Dark days for public discourse," October 31, 2018, https://www.bostonglobe.com/opinion/2018/10/30/dark-days-for-public-discourse/cecK0M8hw3rH2ZflCbWhbK/story.html

**NPR:** Asma Khalid, NPR, "How Massachusetts' Republican Governor Has Remained So Resilient In A Blue State," November 2, 2018, https://www.npr.org/2018/11/02/663655451/how-massachusetts-republican-governor-has-remained-so-resilient-in-a-blue-state

### Three Teen Candidates in Kansas

**ABC News:** Kendall Karson, ABC News, "They can't vote, but these Kansas teens are running for governor," August 7, 2018, https://abcnews.go.com/Politics/vote-kansas-teens-running-governor/story?id=57058542

**Christian Science Monitor:** Christa Case Bryant, *Christian Science Monitor,* "Forget prom king – they're running for governor," April 16, 2018, https://www.csmonitor.com/USA/Politics/2018/0416/Forget-prom-king-they-re-running-for-governor

**Wichita Eagle:** Dion Lefler, *Wichita Eagle*, "If it wasn't for those teens running in the governor's race, would we be in this mess?" August 8, 2018, https://www.kansas.com/news/politics-government/election/article216330705.html

**Cory Booker**

**The Last Show With Stephen Colbert:** Cory Booker, "Sen. Cory Booker Wants A Revival Of Civic Grace," March 8, 2019, https://www.youtube.com/watch?v=ybzt-VJVjClM

**Colbert's show**: Cory Booker, "Sen. Cory Booker Talks Race, Empathy, And His Legislation To Stop Abuses Of Power By Law Enforcement," June 5, 2020, https://www.youtube.com/watch?v=Ayizzcv-NCE

**Jimmy Kimmel Live**: Cory Booker, "Senator Cory Booker Refuses to Hate Donald Trump," May 4, 2018, https://www.youtube.com/watch?v=kRoGR3AYads

**CNBC interview with John Hardwood:** John Hardwood, CNBC, "Democratic presidential candidate Cory Booker walks the line between business and the left," June 13, 2019, https://www.cnbc.com/2019/06/12/democratic-presidential-candi-date-cory-booker-walks-the-line-between-business-and-the-left.html

**CBS:** Emily Tillett, CBS, "Sens. Cory Booker and Mike Lee on putting aside politics to reform criminal justice," July 22, 2019, https://www.cbsnews.com/news/senators-cory-booker-mike-lee-on-putting-aside-political-impasses-to-reform-crim-inal-justice/

**Ruth Buffalo**

**New York Times:** Maggie Astor, *New York Times*, "Meet the Native American Woman Who Beat the Sponsor of North Dakota's ID Law," November 13, 2018, https://www.nytimes.com/2018/11/13/us/politics/north-dakota-ruth-buffalo.html

**Indian Country Today:** Jourdan Bennett Begaye, *Indian Country Today*, "Three North Dakota challenges for Ruth Buffalo: She's a woman. She's Native. And she's a Democrat," April 11, 2019, https://indiancountrytoday.com/news/three-north-dako-ta-challenges-for-ruth-buffalo-she-s-a-woman-she-s-native-and-she-s-a-democrat-p1PlQtg3h0-SwoZvtP7SNA

**High Plains Reader:** Lonnie Whiting, *High Plains Reader*, "RUTH ANNA BUF-FALO: WOMAN OF THE YEAR," October 2, 2019, https://hpr1.com/index.php/feature/news/ruth-anna-buffalo-woman-of-the-year

**Facing Race Awards:** Jim Walsh, MinnPost, "'We really need to get rid of Min-nesota Nice and start having honest conversations': 2019 Facing Race Awards recognize anti-racism activists and leaders," September 20, 2019, https://www.minnpost.com/community-sketchbook/2019/09/we-really-need-to-get-rid-of-min-nesota-nice-and-start-having-honest-conversations-2019-facing-race-awards-recognize-anti-racism-activists-and-leaders/

**Newsweek**: Christina Zhao, *Newsweek,* "Meet Ruth Buffalo, the First Native American Democratic Woman in North Dakota's Statehouse," January 6, 2019, https://www.newsweek.com/meet-first-native-woman-american-democrat-north-dakotas-statehouse-1281196

**Huffington Post:** Carla Herreria Russo, Huffington Post, "First Native Woman Democrat In N.D. Statehouse Takes Oath In Traditional Dress," December 5, 2018, https://www.huffpost.com/entry/ruth-buffalo-north-dakota-traditional-native-american-dress_n_5c06f9a4e4b0680a7ec9dc2d

### G.T. Bynum

**KRMG interview:** Ben Morgan, KRMG, "Tulsa Mayor GT Bynum: 'You saw the middle prevail' during weekend Trump Rally and protests," June 22, 2020, https://www.krmg.com/news/local/tulsa-mayor-bynum-you-saw-the-middle-prevail-during-weekend-trump-rally-and-protests/Fu1QdWLGWtKNV18GZnTRsM/

**Washington Post:** DeNeen L. Brown, *Washington Post,* "A white Republican mayor seeks the truth about Tulsa's race massacre a century ago," March 13, 2020, https://www.washingtonpost.com/history/2020/03/13/tulsa-mayor-bynum-mass-graves/

**TED Talk:** G.T. Bynum, "A Republican Mayor's Plan to Replace Partisanship With Policy," February 2017, https://www.ted.com/talks/g_t_bynum_a_republican_mayor_s_plan_to_replace_partisanship_with_policy

**Tulsa World:** G.T. Bynum, *Tulsa World*, "Outlook 2020: Mayor G.T. Bynum: Building a Tulsa to be proud of," March 1, 2020, https://tulsaworld.com/news/local/outlook-2020-mayor-g-t-bynum-building-a-tulsa-to-be-proud-of/article_6b1e246b-d35f-5513-87e4-5ce28d05725a.html

### Dan Crenshaw

**Washington Post op-ed**: Dan Crenshaw, *Washington Post*, "SNL mocked my appearance, here's why I didn't demand an apology," November 13, 2018, https://www.washingtonpost.com/opinions/i-made-amends-with-pete-davidson-on-snl-but-thats-only-the-beginning/2018/11/13/e7314fb0-e77e-11e8-b8dc-66cca409c180_story.html

**Conservative Political Action Conference speech:** John McCormick, POLITICO, "Is Dan Crenshaw the Future of the GOP?," March 2, 2019, https://www.politico.com/magazine/story/2019/03/02/is-dan-crenshaw-the-future-of-the-gop-225257

**said in the midst of COVID-19:** Claire Goodman, *Houston Chronicle*, "SUNDAY CONVERSATION: Dan Crenshaw reflects on lessons from COVID-19, plans future flood mitigation strategies," May 20, 2020, https://www.chron.com/

neighborhood/katy/news/article/SUNDAY-CONVERSATION-Dan-Crenshaw-reflects-on-15257331.php

**New York Times:** Lisa Lerer, *New York Times,* "On Politics With Lisa Lerer: A Chat With Dan Crenshaw," February 21, 2019, https://www.nytimes.com/2019/02/21/us/politics/on-politics-dan-crenshaw.html

**The View:** Charlotte Alter, Viking, *The Ones We've Been Waiting For: How a New Generation of Leaders Will Transform America,* 2020.

**The Ones We've Been Waiting For:** Charlotte Alter, Viking, *The Ones We've Been Waiting For: How a New Generation of Leaders Will Transform America,* 2020.

**opinion piece:** Dan Crenshaw, The Hill, "What to us is the Fourth of July?" July 4, 2020, https://thehill.com/blogs/congress-blog/politics/505853-what-to-us-is-the-fourth-of-july

**graduation speech:** Sean Neumann, *People,* "Texas Lawmaker Tells Students to 'Embrace Hardship' in a 'Real World' Coronavirus Commencement Speech," May 28, 2020, https://people.com/politics/texas-rep-dan-crenshaw-tells-students-embrace-hardship-commencement-speech/

### Carlos Curbelo

**The Hill:** Kyle Balluck, The Hill, "Republican Fla. rep calls for debate on 'gun safety laws'," February 18, 2018, https://thehill.com/homenews/sunday-talk-shows/374436-republican-fla-rep-calls-for-debate-on-gun-safety-laws

**Miami Herald:** Carlos Curbelo, *Miami Herald,* "Climate change cannot be a partisan issue," October 24, 2015, https://www.miamiherald.com/opinion/op-ed/article41324724.html

**ABC News:** Benjamin Siegel andJohn Parkinson, ABC News, "House rejects Republican compromise immigration bill," June 27, 2018, https://abcnews.go.com/Politics/house-rejects-republican-compromise-immigration-bill/story?id=56200199

**The Ones We've Been Waiting For:** Charlotte Alter, Viking, *The Ones We've Been Waiting For: How a New Generation of Leaders Will Transform America,* 2020.

**Cuomo Prime Time:** Carlos Curbelo, Twitter, November 2, 2018, https://twitter.com/CuomoPrimeTime/status/1058540172352974848

**The Hill:** Juliegrace Brufke, The Hill, "Disinvited GOP lawmaker turns up at Dem hearing," May 15, 2019, https://thehill.com/homenews/house/443823-disinvited-gop-lawmaker-turns-up-at-dem-hearing

**Tammy Duckworth**

**Chicago Magazine**: Carol Felsenthal, *Chicago Magazine*, "'Nothing to Lose': Tammy Duckworth on Her Quest to Go to Congress," May 11, 2012, https://www. chicagomag.com/Chicago-Magazine/Felsenthal-Files/May-2012/Tammy-Duck-worth-on-her-Quest-to-Go-to-Congress-Nothing-to-Lose/

**Chicago Tribune**: *Chicago Tribune*, "Celebrating 'Alive Day'," November 23, 2006, https://www.chicagotribune.com/news/ct-xpm-2006-11-23-0611230042-story.html

**NPR**: Ailsa Chang, NPR, "Illinois Sen. Tammy Duckworth On Her First Meeting With Sen. John McCain,"August 27, 2018, https://www.npr. org/2018/08/27/642356449/illinois-sen-tammy-duckworth-on-her-first-meeting-with-sen-john-mccain

**Maia Espinoza**

**KUOW:** Amy Radil, KUOW, "'We don't really do P.C.' Latino liberals and conserva-tives converge in Seattle," January 17, 2020, https://www.kuow.org/stories/for-lati-no-leaders-event-in-seattle-a-bipartisan-lineup-and-blunt-conversation

**The Lily:** Torey Van Oot, The Lily, "They are part of the wave of millennial women seeking office. The difference? They are Republican." November 5, 2018, https:// www.thelily.com/they-are-part-of-the-wave-of-millennial-women-seeking-office-the-difference-they-are-republican/

**Crosscut:** Cambria Roth, Crosscut, "She's 29, Latina and running for office — as a Republican," October 10, 2018, https://crosscut.com/2018/10/shes-29-lati-na-and-running-office-republican

**KIRO story:** Dori Monson, KIRO, "Sex ed bill inspired activist Maia Espinoza to run for superintendent," March 9, 2020, https://mynorthwest.com/1755083/dori-maia-espinoza-superintendent/?

**2018 KIRO story:** Dori Monson, KIRO, "Maia Espinoza aims to bring diversity to Republicans in state Legislature," October 25, 2018, https://mynorthwest. com/1159156/maia-espinoza-state-legislature/?

**Beth Fukumoto**

**Letter:** Beth Fukumoto, "A Letter to Republicans," March 22, 2017 https://bethfu-kumoto.com/a-letter-to-republicans-my-party-resignation/

**TIME:** Samantha Cooney, *TIME*, "GOP Rep Who Left Party Felt 'Racism and Sexism Coming Into Play,'" March 23, 2017, https://time.com/4711664/beth-fukumo-to-republicans-sexism-interview/

**NBC:** Emil Guillermo, NBC, "In Hawaii Republican Caucus, a Fight for the GOP's

Future," March 7, 2016, https://www.nbcnews.com/news/asian-america/hawaii-republican-caucus-fight-gop-s-future-n533576

**The Cut**: Claire Landsbaum, The Cut, "Hawaii House Republican Leader Pushed Out After Speaking at the Women's March," February 3, 2017, https://www.thecut.com/2017/02/hawaii-republican-leader-ousted-after-womens-march-speech.html

*Elle:* Melissa Harris-Perry, *Elle*, "Hawaii State Rep. Beth Fukumoto Explains Why She Might Leave The Republican Party," February 10, 2017, https://www.elle.com/culture/career-politics/a42949/hawaii-beth-fukumoto-leaving-republican-party/

**Video resigning**: Beth Fukumoto, "Announcement to Leave the Republican Party," March 22, 2017, https://www.youtube.com/watch?v=s0t2WSWmQ9I

*Glamour:* Celeste Katz, *Glamour*, "For Female Political Candidates, Sometimes the Biggest Threat Isn't Losing an Election," September 17, 2018, https://www.glamour.com/story/female-political-candidates-verbal-harassment-threats-midterms

**Women's March speech:** Beth Fukumoto, "2017 Hawai'i Women's March," January 21, 2017 https://www.youtube.com/watch?v=2QIoaDvP_bw

**Justin Giboney**

*Christianity Today*: Justin Giboney, *Christianity Today*, "How Urban Christians Failed President Obama," May 26, 2016, https://www.christianitytoday.com/ct/2016/may-web-only/how-urban-christians-failed-president-obama.html

**Catholic News Agency:** Kevin J. Jones, Catholic News Agency, "Lonely but determined, pro-life Democrats speak up," July 31, 2018, https://www.catholicnewsagency.com/news/lonely-but-determined-pro-life-democrats-speak-up-51099

*Christian Post:* Samuel Smith, *Christian Post*, "Democrat Strategist Said He Received Pushback for Urging Party to Welcome Biblical Values," June 19, 2018, https://www.christianpost.com/news/democrat-strategist-received-pushback-urging-party-welcome-biblical-values-justin-giboney-and-campaign.html

**The Hill:** Justin Giboney, The Hill, "Our self-defeating politics of pettiness serves no good," February 7, 2020, https://thehill.com/opinion/campaign/481636-our-self-defeating-politics-of-pettiness-serves-no-good

**"Lethal Mass Partisanship":** Nathan P. Kalmoe and Lilliana Mason, "Lethal Mass Partisanship," January 2019, https://www.dannyhayes.org/uploads/6/9/8/5/69858539/kalmoe__mason_ncapsa_2019_-_lethal_partisanship_-_final_lmedit.pdf

**online video:** Justin Giboney, "Do You Hate Your Political Opponents?" March 29, 2019, https://www.thecruxandthecall.com/civic-updates/2019/3/29/civicupdate-do-you-hate-your-political-opponents

**Detroit Catholic:** Catholic News Service, Detroit Catholic, "Panel: At ballot box, let Gospel, not a political party, guide your vote," October 11, 2019, https://detroit-catholic.com/news/catholic-news-service/panel-at-ballot-box-let-gospel-not-a-political-party-guide-your-vote

***World Magazine:*** Marvin Olasky, *World Magazine*, "Christian and Democrat," December 12, 2019, https://world.wng.org/2019/12/christian_and_democrat

**Twitter:** Luke Bobo, Twitter, December 11, 2019, https://twitter.com/lukebbobo1/status/1204822995056939008

### Jenean Hampton

**crowd in western Kentucky:** John Gregory, KET's Connections, "Lieutenant Governor Candidate Jenean Hampton Profile," 2015, https://www.ket.org/program/connections-with-renee-shaw-lt-governors-race/jenean-hampton/

**WDRB interview:** Lawrence Smith, WDRB, "Ky. Lt. Gov. Jenean Hampton says she did not vote for Gov. Matt Bevin," November 26, 2019, https://www.wdrb.com/news/ky-lt-gov-jenean-hampton-says-she-did-not-vote/article_c44b4a48-106b-11ea-9e96-6f1645e4cf16.html

***Louisville Courier Journal:*** Phillip M. Bailey, *Louisville Courier Journal*, "Matt Bevin's running mate: I'm just 'Jenean,'" October 9, 2015, https://www.courier-journal.com/story/news/politics/2015/10/09/matt-bevins-running-mate-m-just-jenean/73145924/

**WBKO interview:** WBKO News Staff, WBKO, "Lieutenant Governor Jenean Hampton celebrates 200th school visit," October 17, 2019, https://www.wbko.com/content/news/Lieutenant-Governor-Jenean-Hampton-celebrates-200th-school-visit-563314822.html

**WKYT interview:** Hillary Thornton, WKYT, "Hampton on final year in office: 'If we were doing a TV series, no one would believe it,'" December 3, 2019, https://www.wkyt.com/content/news/Hampton-on-final-year-in-office-If-we-were-doing-a-TV-series-no-one-would-believe-it-565734092.html

### Caleb Hanna

***Charleston Gazette Mail:*** Susan Matthis Johnson, *Charleston Gazette Mail,* "Youngest black legislator in America ready to get to work for WV," January 6, 2019, https://www.wvgazettemail.com/life/youngest-black-legislator-in-america-ready-to-get-to-work/article_9f22e066-ab68-5f18-90be-a79fe0868dfc.html

**tweeted**: Caleb Hanna, Twitter, December 13, 2017, https://twitter.com/Delegate-Hanna/status/941065383888457729

***New York Times:*** Adeel Hassan, *New York Times*, "Freshman in College, Freshman in the Capitol: West Virginia's 19-Year-Old Lawmaker," January 27, 2019, https://www.nytimes.com/2019/01/27/us/caleb-hanna-bio-facts-republican-gop.html

**West Virginia State**: West Virginia State, "Yellow Jacket in the House," April 17, 2019, https://issuu.com/wvsupublications/docs/state_magazine_vol_7_2019_041819_fi

**Tennessee Star:** Evie Fordham, *Tennessee Star,* "Youngest Black Legislator In America Won on a Platform of 'God, Guns, and Babies,'" January 15, 2019, https://tennesseestar.com/2019/01/15/youngest-black-legislator-in-america-won-on-a-plat-form-of-god-guns-and-babies/

**Register-Herald:** Pat Hanna, *Register Herald,* "One for the (young) ages; Nicholas County college students ace election tests, prepare to take office," November 18, 2018, https://www.register-herald.com/news/life/one-for-the-young-ages-nicholas-county-college-students-ace-election-tests-prepare-to-take/article_47bc0cc7-592c-5bc6-baf3-4427094d94b8.html

### Jaime Herrera Beutler

**The Hill**: Tess Bonn, The Hill, "GOP lawmaker looks to address racial disparities in maternal mortality rates," June 18, 2018, https://thehill.com/business-a-lobby-ing/392797-rep-jaime-herrera-beutler-looks-to-address-disparities-maternal-mortality

**CNN:** Dana Bash, CNN, "How Rep. Herrera Beutler saved her baby," June 12, 2017, https://www.cnn.com/2017/06/12/politics/jaime-herrera-beutler-badass-wom-en-of-washington/index.html

**editorial:** Jaime Herrera Beutler and Raja Krishnamoorthi, The Hill, "Alone among developed nations, the US maternal mortality rate is rising. Here's how we can fix that," July 26, 2018, https://thehill.com/blogs/congress-blog/healthcare/398860-alone-among-developed-nations-the-us-maternal-mortality-rate

**POLITICO**: Rishika Dugyala and Melanie Zanona, POLITICO, "Can the Repub-lican Party Save One of Its Last Latina Congresswomen?" December 11, 2019, https://www.politico.com/news/magazine/2019/12/11/can-the-republican-par-ty-save-its-only-latina-voting-congresswoman-076693

### Adam Kinzinger

**Weekly Standard:** Michael Warren, *Weekly Standard,* "Adam Kinzinger, Rising Republican Star," July 6, 2012, https://www.washingtonexaminer.com/weekly-stan-dard/adam-kinzinger-rising-republican-star

**CNN:** Naomi Lim, CNN, "GOP congressman says he can't support Trump: 'I'm an American before I'm a Republican'," August 3, 2016, https://www.cnn.com/2016/08/03/politics/election-2016-adam-kinzinger-american-before-a-repub-lican/index.html

**Esquire**: Mark Warren, *Esquire*, "Profiles in Congress: Representative Adam Kinzinger," October 15, 2014, https://www.esquire.com/news-politics/news/a30299/profiles-in-congress-representative-adam-kinzinger/

**TMZ:** Adam Kinzinger, TMZ, "Rep. Adam Kinzinger: Gun Laws Have to Change," August 6, 2019, https://www.tmz.com/2019/08/06/congressman-adam-kinzinger-dayton-el-paso-shooting-gun-control-laws/

### Brenda Kupchick

**Fairfield Citizen:** Rachel Scharf, *Fairfield Citizen*, "Kupchick sworn in as Fairfield's First Selectwoman," November 27, 2019 https://www.fairfieldcitizenonline.com/news/article/Kupchick-sworn-in-as-Fairfield-s-First-14862602.php

**Fairfield Citizen:** Rachel Scharf, *Fairfield Citizen*, "Inside Kupchick's plans for bringing accountability back to Fairfield," November 12, 2019, https://www.fairfield-citizenonline.com/news/article/Inside-Kupchick-s-plans-for-bringing-14828948.php

**Connecticut News 12:** Connecticut News 12, "State Rep. Kupchick eager to begin work as Fairfield's 2nd first selectwoman," November 13, 2019, http://connecticut.news12.com/story/41316000/state-rep-kupchick-eager-to-begin-work-as-fairfields-2nd-first-selectwoman

**Westfair:** Kevin Zimmerman, Westfair, "Fairfield First Selectwoman Brenda Kupchick: Time to right the ship is now," January 12, 2020, https://westfaironline.com/120090/fairfield-1st-selectwoman-brenda-kupchick-time-to-right-the-ship-is-now/

**Fairfield Citizen:** Rachel Scharf, *Fairfield Citizen*, "Kupchick gets up to speed, hires staff in week one as Fairfield First Selectwoman," December 4, 2019, https://www.fairfieldcitizenonline.com/news/article/Kupchick-gets-up-to-speed-hires-staff-in-week-14881955.php

### Cassandra Levesque

**New York Times:** Kate Taylor, *New York Times*, "In New Class of Young Lawmakers, a Former Girl Scout Goes to the Statehouse," November 13, 2018, https://www.nytimes.com/2018/11/13/us/young-candidates-elections.html

**said:** Jewel Wicker, *Teen Vogue*, "19-Year-Old Election Winner Cassandra Levesque Is Ready to Shake Up New Hampshire's State Legislature, the Oldest in the Country," December 5, 2018, https://www.teenvogue.com/story/19-year-old-election-winner-cassandra-levesque-new-hampshires-state-legislature-shake-up

**Girl Scout profile:** Cassandra Levesque, GirlScouts.org, "At Girl Scouts, We Change Laws. We Change the World: Cassie Levesque," September 18, 2019, https://www.girlscouts.org/en/about-girl-scouts/our-stories/alumnae/why-girl-scouts-cassie-levesque.html

**Twitter:** Cassandra Levesque, Twitter, November 30, 2018, https://twitter.com/Cassandra4NH/status/1068480466708299777

**The Concord Monitor:** Leah Willingham, *The Concord Monitor*, "Teen rep. pushes to raise NH marriage age again," February 24, 2019, https://www.fosters.com/news/20190224/teen-rep-pushes-to-raise-nh-marriage-age-again

**Duke University event:** Hannah Miao, Duke Today, "Balancing College Life With Being an Elected Legislator," April 2, 2019, https://today.duke.edu/2019/04/balancing-college-life-being-elected-legislator

**Barrington Town News:** Patrick R. McElhiney, *Barrington Town News*, "Interview with State Rep. Cassandra Levesque," September 22, 2019, https://www.barringtontownnews.com/index.php/articles-2/196-interview-with-state-rep-cassandra-levesque

**Boston Globe:** Dialynn Dwyer, *Boston Globe*, "'Keep fighting for something that you believe in': Meet the 19-year-old who is headed to the New Hampshire State House," December 4, 2018, https://www.boston.com/news/politics/2018/12/04/cassandra-levesque-new-hampshire-state-representative

## Jeff Lunde

**The Hill:** Reid Wilson, The Hill, "Six mayors making a difference," January 22, 2020, https://thehill.com/homenews/state-watch/479257-six-mayors-making-a-difference

**press release:** Rep. Dean Phillips, "Phillips Invites Brooklyn Park Mayor Jeff Lunde to State of the Union," January 29, 2020, https://phillips.house.gov/media/press-releases/phillips-invites-brooklyn-park-mayor-jeff-lunde-state-union

**Sun Post:** Kevin Miller, *Sun Post*, "Lunde reflects on trip to State of the Union," February 11, 2020, https://www.hometownsource.com/sun_post/community/brooklynpark/lunde-reflects-on-trip-to-state-of-the-union/article_2a130d46-4ce6-11ea-b14c-df1e05cc07b2.html

**Star Tribune:** Shannon Prather, *Star Tribune*, "Brooklyn Park mayor calls for unity in wake of anti-Muslim rhetoric," December 29, 2015, https://www.startribune.com/brooklyn-park-mayor-calls-for-unity-in-wake-of-anti-muslim-rhetoric/363769371/

## Matt Little

**Star Tribune:** Matt Little, *Star Tribune*, "Counterpoint: Door-knocking is heart and soul of healthy democracy," February 18, 2020, https://www.startribune.com/counterpoint-door-knocking-is-heart-and-soul-of-healthy-democracy/567985132/

**tweeted:** Matt Little, Twitter, July 4, 2018, https://twitter.com/LittleSenator/status/1014632139881672706

**POLITICO:** Max Cohen, POLITICO, "Meet The Politician Who Lives on TikTok," August 14, 2020, https://www.politico.com/news/magazine/2020/08/14/politicians-using-tiktok-matt-little-395620

**tweeted:** Matt Little, Twitter, July 15, 2020, https://twitter.com/LittleSenator/status/1283398217443549186

## Lisa Murkowski

***Press Herald:*** Associated Press, *Press Herald*, "Murkowski regrets voting with GOP on birth control," March 10, 2012, https://www.pressherald.com/2012/03/10/murkowski-regrets-voting-with-gop-on-birth-control/

***TIME:*** Jay Newton-Small, *TIME*, "Murkowski's Renegade Run: 'I'm Not Going to Quit on My State,'" September 24, 2010, http://content.time.com/time/politics/article/0,8599,2021245,00.html

**Katie Couric in 2010:** JoAnne Allen, Reuters, "Murkowski rates write-in campaign courageous or crazy," November 16, 2010, http://blogs.reuters.com/talesfromthetrail/2010/11/16/murkowski-rates-write-in-campaign-courageous-or-crazy/

**Real Clear Politics:** John King, Real Clear Politics, "Interview with Senator Lisa Murkowski," November 12, 2010, https://www.realclearpolitics.com/articles/2010/11/12/interview_with_senator_lisa_murkowski_107954.html

***Washington Post:*** Steven Mufson, *Washington Post*, "Q&A: Republican Sen. Lisa Murkowski of Alaska on her '20/20' vision for energy policy," February 9, 2013, https://www.washingtonpost.com/business/qanda-republican-sen-lisa-murkowski-of-alaska-on-her-2020-vision-for-energy-policy/2013/02/08/48530f0e-6f35-11e2-8b8d-e0b59a1b8e2a_story.html

***Anchorage Daily News:*** Erika Bolstad, *Anchorage Daily News,* "Lisa Murkowski: Walking a fine line," October 27, 2010, https://www.adn.com/alaska-news/article/lisa-murkowski-walking-fine-line/2010/10/28/

**NBC:** Phil Helsel and Frank Thorp V, NBC, "Why Murkowski, still opposed, will be marked 'present' on Kavanaugh," October 5, 2018, https://www.nbcnews.com/politics/politics-news/why-murkowski-still-opposed-will-be-marked-present-kavanaugh-n917306

**described:** Lauren Fox, Manu Raju and Ali Zaslav, CNN, "GOP senator says she's 'struggling' on whether to back Trump," June 4, 2020, https://www.cnn.com/2020/06/04/politics/lisa-murkowski-mattis-trump-reaction/index.html

**Real Clear Politics:** John King, Real Clear Politics, "Interview with Senator Lisa Murkowski," October 10, 2010, https://www.realclearpolitics.com/articles/2010/10/20/interview_with_senator_lisa_murkowski_107672.html

### Svante Myrick

**Governing.com:** Caroline Cournoyer, Governing.com, "Millennials in the Mayor's Seat," January 2013, https://www.governing.com/topics/politics/gov-millennial-mayors.html

*The Ones We've Been Waiting For:* Charlotte Alter, Viking, *The Ones We've Been Waiting For: How a New Generation of Leaders Will Transform America,* 2020.

**Cornell alumni magazine:** Beth Saulnier, *Cornell,* "Mr. Mayor," http://cornellalumnimagazine.com/mr-mayor/

*TIME:* Charlotte Alter, *TIME,* 'We Can Do it Better.' Meet the Millennials Taking Over City Hall," October 12, 2017, https://time.com/4979264/meet-millennials-taking-over-city-hall/

**Visit Ithaca interview:** Visit Ithaca, https://www.visitithaca.com/blog/ithaca-people-svante-myrick

### Collin Peterson

**Twitter:** Collin Peterson, Twitter, August 8, 2014, https://twitter.com/collinpeterson/status/497837442762694656

*Fergus Falls Journal:* Forum News Service, *Fergus Falls Journal,* "Study: Rep. Peterson ranks first in bipartisan legislation," April 26, 2018, https://www.fergusfallsjournal.com/news/study-rep-peterson-ranks-first-in-bipartisan-legislation/article_41f8fce3-9f2e-5b4d-bdd9-a79143141bb0.html

*Star Tribune:* Patrick Condon, *Star Tribune,* "Guns back on the agenda as Congress returns," September 9, 2019, https://www.startribune.com/guns-back-on-the-agenda-as-congress-returns/559828882/

**MPR:** Dan Gunderson, MPR News, "Collin Peterson to seek reelection in Minnesota's 7th District," March 6, 2020, https://www.mprnews.org/story/2020/03/06/collin-peterson-to-seek-reelection-in-minnesotas-7th-district

**statement about his vote:** Collin Peterson, FOX 9, "Minnesota's Rep. Collin Peterson calls impeachment a 'mistake,' is one of 2 Democratic 'no' votes," December 18, 2019, https://www.mprnews.org/story/2020/03/06/collin-peterson-to-seek-reelection-in-minnesotas-7th-district

**MinnPost:** Sam Brodey, Minn Post, "Collin Peterson explains his 'Give Trump the money' remarks: 'I'm probably the only one left that has the guts to say what I said,'" January 23, 2019, https://www.minnpost.com/national/2019/01/collin-peter-son-explains-his-give-trump-the-money-remarks-im-probably-the-only-one-left-that-has-the-guts-to-say-what-i-said/

**National Grain and Feed Association:** National Grain and Feed Association, "House Agriculture Committee Chairman Collin Peterson talks farm bill and trade priorities with NGFA," March 8, 2019, https://www.ngfa.org/newsletter/house-ag-riculture-committee-chairman-collin-peterson-talks-farm-bill-and-trade-priori-ties-with-ngfa/

**POLITICO:** Liz Crampton, POLITICO, "GOP seeks to dethrone Collin Peterson, one of the Hill's few rural Democrats," November 11, 2019, https://www.politico.com/news/2019/11/11/minnesota-collin-peterson-rural-democrats-068016

### Jared Polis

**inaugural speech:** Mike Littwin, Colorado Springs Indy, "Jared Polis, and Colorado voters, make history," January 16, 2019, https://www.csindy.com/coloradosprings/jared-polis-and-colorado-voters-make-history/Content?oid=18115346

**poem:** Brett T., Twitchy, "'What a sham!' Rep. Jared Polis pens an anti-Cruz, anti-shutdown poem," September 28, 2013, https://twitchy.com/brettt-3136/2013/09/28/what-a-sham-rep-jared-polis-pens-an-anti-cruz-anti-shut-down-poem/

**inauguration:** Blair Miller, Denver ABC, January 8, 2019, https://www.thedenver-channel.com/news/politics/make-colorado-work-for-everyone-democrat-jared-po-lis-sworn-in-as-colorados-43rd-governor

**emailed supporters a poem:** Huffington Post, "Jared Polis Poetry: Polis Reflects On The New Year In Verse," March 18, 2010, https://www.huffpost.com/entry/jar-ed-polis-poetry-polis_n_407262

**Democratic National Convention:** (Ret.) Gen. Jim Jones, POLITICO, "Jared Polis DNC speech (text)," September 4, 2012, https://www.politico.com/story/2012/09/jared-polis-dnc-speech-text-080702

**Fox News:** Neil Cavuto, Fox News, "Rep. Polis talks Democratic base's protests against Trump," February 2, 2017, https://www.foxnews.com/transcript/rep-polis-talks-democratic-bases-protests-against-trump

**2020 State of the State speech:** Kara Mason, *Sentinel,* "POLIS: 'We don't build walls of exclusion, we build ladders of opportunity'," January 9, 2020, https://sen-tinelcolorado.com/news/state-and-region/gov-polis/

### Qasim Rashid

**CBS News:** Steve Hartman, CBS News, "A man sent a hateful message to a Muslim candidate. He responded with a call for help," March 13, 2020, https://www.cbsnews.com/news/a-man-sent-a-hateful-message-to-a-muslim-candidate-he-responded-with-a-call-to-help/

**tweeted:** Qasim Rashid, Twitter, February 23, 2020 https://twitter.com/QasimRashid/status/1231605783479115783

**friend:** Qasim Rashid, Twitter, March 8, 2020, https://twitter.com/QasimRashid/status/1236844264472051712

**NBC News:** Janelle Griffith, NBC News, "Man sent anti-Muslim tweets to a political candidate who then helped pay his medical debt," March 10, 2020, https://www.nbcnews.com/news/us-news/man-sent-anti-muslim-tweets-political-candidate-who-then-helped-n1154581

**PRI:** Rupa Shenoy, The World, "This Muslim American congressional candidate sees hateful messages as a chance for dialogue," March 18, 2020, https://www.pri.org/stories/2020-03-18/muslim-american-congressional-candidate-sees-hateful-messages-chance-dialogue

## Regina Romero

**inauguration:** Valerie Cavazos, KGUN 9, "Tucson's first Latina mayor Regina Romero sworn in Monday," December 1, 2019, https://www.kgun9.com/news/local-news/tucsons-first-female-latina-mayor-regina-romero-to-be-sworn-in-monday

**Telemundo:** Telemundo, "Regina Romero quiere ser la primera alcaldesa latina de Tucson y "limpiar la imagen" anti-inmigrante de Arizona," November 5, 2019, https://www.telemundo.com/noticias/2019/11/05/regina-romero-quiere-ser-la-primera-alcaldesa-latina-de-tucson-y-limpiar-la-imagen-anti-tmna3574551

**KGUN:** KGUN 9 On Your Side, KGUN 9, "Tucson Mayor Regina Romero speaks out against proposed sanctuary city ban in Arizona," February 19, 2020, https://www.kgun9.com/news/local-news/tucson-mayor-regina-romero-speaks-out-against-proposed-sanctuary-city-ban-in-arizona

**Phoenix:** Jimmy Magahern, Phoenix, "Who's the Boss?" January 23, 2020, https://www.phoenixmag.com/2020/01/23/whos-the-boss/

**AZPM:** Kassandra Lau, AZPM, "Journalists roundtable, Regina Romero, free speech at the UA," August 30, 2019, https://www.azpm.org/s/69474-journalists-roundtable-regina-romero-free-speech-at-the-ua/

**AZPM:** Arizona 360, AZPM, "Tucson Mayor-elect Regina Romero lays out immediate priorities," November 8, 2019, https://www.azpm.org/p/azill-home/2019/11/8/161487-tucson-mayor-elect-regina-romero-lays-out-immediate-priorities/

**Tucson.com:** Joe Ferguson, Tucson.com, "Mayor-elect Romero says expanding KIDCO afterschool program will be a top priority," November 7, 2019, https://tucson.com/news/local/mayor-elect-romero-says-expanding-kidco-afterschool-program-will-be-a-top-priority/article_d58680d4-2ebe-5a8c-934e-58aa54a3e3ed.html

**Tucson.com:** Joe Ferguson, Tucson.com, "Political Notebook: Democrat Romero's campaign co-chair donated to Trump in 2016," July 25, 2019, https://tucson.com/news/local/political-notebook-democrat-romeros-campaign-co-chair-donated-to-trump-in-2016/article_b36f9e9a-3c28-5461-90a6-62b19f210cce.html

**KGUN:** Phil Villarreal, KGUN 9, "Mayor creates racial equity, justice advisory board," June 10, 2020, https://www.kgun9.com/news/local-news/mayor-creates-racial-equity-justice-advisory-board

**inauguration:** Joe Ferguson, This Is Tucson, "Regina Romero becomes first Latina to serve as Tucson's mayor," November 6, 2019, https://thisistucson.com/news/local/govt-and-politics/regina-romero-becomes-first-latina-to-serve-as-tucson-s/article_66dddb7a-0042-11ea-bb64-1fdf625b36b4.html#tracking-source=home-top-story-1

### Max Rose

**POLITICO:** Michael Kruse, POLITICO, "'If We Beat Covid and He Wins Reelection, So Be It,'" April 17, 2020, https://www.politico.com/news/magazine/2020/04/17/interview-max-rose-covid-193258

**POLITICO:** Michael Kruse, POLITICO, "How Veterans Are Powering the Democrats' 2018 Hopes," March 28, 2018, https://www.politico.com/magazine/story/2018/03/28/midterms-veterans-millennial-democrats-gop-districts-217714

***The Ones We've Been Waiting For:*** Charlotte Alter, Viking, *The Ones We've Been Waiting For: How a New Generation of Leaders Will Transform America*, 2020.

**Twitter:** Max Rose, Twitter, May 5, 2020, https://twitter.com/RepMaxRose/status/1257730705712394249

**SILive.com:** Pearl Minsky, *Staten Island Advance*, "Memoirs: Congressman Max Rose," November 11, 2018, https://www.silive.com/news/2019/11/memoirs-congressman-max-rose.html

**SILive.com:** Kristin F. Dalton: Staten Island Advance, "'We still have work to do,' Rep. Rose said during reelection campaign kickoff at The Vanderbilt," February 8, 2020, https://www.silive.com/news/2020/02/we-still-have-work-to-do-rep-rose-said-during-reelection-campaign-kickoff-at-the-vanderbilt.html

### Ben Sasse

**in a clip reminiscent of late night TV:** Mark Hensch, The Hill, "GOP senator reads mean tweets from Trump fans," February 18, 2016, https://thehill.com/blogs/in-the-know/in-the-know/269847-gop-senator-reads-mean-tweets-from-trump-fans

**drive for Uber:** Marguerite Ward, CNBC, "This U.S. senator drives for Uber to find out what his constituents really think,"November 17, 2016, https://www.cnbc.com/2016/11/17/why-this-gop-senator-also-drives-for-uber.html

**Twitter:** Ben Sasse, Twitter, November 13, 2016, https://twitter.com/BenSasse/status/797826400447299584

**The Late Show With Stephen Colbert:** Ben Sasse, *The Late Show With Stephen Colbert,* "Senator Ben Sasse: Congress Isn't Working," November 20, 2018, https://www.youtube.com/watch?v=oKKJUHd_XIM

**NPR:** Audie Cornish, *All Things Considered,* "In 'Them,' Sen. Ben Sasse Says Politics Are Not What's Dividing Americans," October 15, 2018, https://www.npr.org/2018/10/15/657588629/in-them-sen-ben-sasse-says-politics-are-not-what-s-dividing-americans

**State of the Union With Jake Tapper:** Joseph Morton, *Omaha World-Herald,* "Ben Sasse, asked about possible party change: 'I conceive of myself as an independent conservative,'" September 10, 2018, https://omaha.com/news/politics/ben-sasse-asked-about-possible-party-change-i-conceive-of/article_c47fdfeb-7958-5906-90d9-e26e25a1b922.html

**Them: Why We Hate Each Other and How to Heal:** Ben Sasse, St. Martin's Press, *Them: Why We Hate Each Other and How to Heal,* 2018.

### Hillary Schieve

**Elle:** Mattie Kahn, *Elle,* "The Nonpartisan Mayor Revitalizing Reno," August 11, 2017, https://www.elle.com/culture/career-politics/news/a47318/hillary-schieve-mayor-reno/

**POLITICO:** Megan Messerly, POLITICO, "America's 11 Most Interesting Mayors," June 25, 2017, https://www.politico.com/magazine/story/2017/06/25/most-interesting-mayors-america-215295

**Common Edge:** Trinity Simons, Arch Daily, "Reno Mayor Hillary Schieve: Burning Man 'Changed Me Forever,'" May 16, 2020, https://www.archdaily.com/939533/reno-mayor-hillary-schieve-burning-man-changed-me-forever

**TEDx Speech:** Hillary Schieve, TEDx Reno, "Why We Should Know Our Local Government," July 7, 2020, https://www.youtube.com/watch?v=d6muMzwVEl4

### Pat Spearman

**responded:** Steve Sebelius, *Las Vegas Review Journal,* "Champion for Equality,"

February 21, 2020, https://www.reviewjournal.com/news/politics-and-government/nevada/for-pat-spearman-the-fight-for-equality-is-the-fight-of-her-life-1961701/

**Huffington Post:** Emily Peck, Huffington Post, "Yes, Virginia! Women Could Finally Get An Equal Rights Amendment," November 6, 2019, https://www.huffpost.com/entry/virginia-equal-rights-amendment-women_n_5dc2f5c4e4b0f5dcf8fef195

**CBS News:** CBS News, "First majority-female legislature pushing for change in Nevada," June 1, 2019, https://www.cbsnews.com/news/majority-female-legislature-pushing-for-change-in-nevada-2019-06-01/

**Elise Stefanik**

**TIME:** Elise Stefanik, *TIME*, "Elise Stefanik: My Advice to Anyone Who's Ever Been the Youngest Woman in the Room," February 5, 2016, https://time.com/4192663/elise-stefanik-young-women-advice/

**USA Today:** Elise Stefanik, *USA Today*, "I was the youngest woman in Congress. Here's my advice to those who have taken my place," January 4, 2019, https://www.usatoday.com/story/opinion/voices/2019/01/04/ocasio-cortez-finkenauer-youngest-women-female-congress-elected-history-column/2473768002/

**tweeted:** Elise Stefanik, Twitter, December 4, 2018, https://twitter.com/EliseStefanik/status/1069950316483874816

**City & State:** Kayla Webley Adler, City & State, "Elise Stefanik wants the unthinkable: more women in the GOP," November 17, 2019, https://www.cityandstateny.com/articles/personality/interviews-profiles/elise-stefanik-wants-the-unthinkable-more-women-in-the-gop.html

**traded barbs:** Shane Croucher, *TIME*, "Alexandria Ocasio-Cortez Told to 'Do Better' by GOP Congresswoman: 'Instead of Lifting Women up Regardless of Party, You Chose to Push Us Down,'" February 7, 2019, https://www.newsweek.com/alexandria-ocasio-cortez-twitter-women-elise-stefanik-1321495

**tweeted:** Elise Stefanik, Twitter, February 6, 2019, https://twitter.com/EliseStefanik/status/1093333161168261120

**Erin Stewart**

**Hartford Courant:** Don Stacom, *Hartford Courant,* "No longer the youngest candidate, New Britain Mayor Erin Stewart runs for fourth term," October 18, 2019, https://www.courant.com/community/new-britain/hc-news-new-britain-erin-stewart-20191018-lylvfozd25hvfbezbu6uk6stiu-story.html

**TIME:** Charlotte Alter, *TIME*, "'We Can Do it Better.' Meet the Millennials Taking Over City Hall," October 12, 2017, https://time.com/4979264/meet-millennials-taking-over-city-hall/

**study:** Mike Maciag, Governing.com, "Mayors Are Harassed and Threatened, But Just How Often?" September 2019, https://www.governing.com/topics/politics/gov-targeting-mayor.html

**Hartford Courant:** Don Stacom and Rebecca Lurye, *Hartford Courant*, "Former Democratic state official posts Facebook insult about Mayor Erin Stewart; she calls attacks 'pathetic, disturbing,'" October 21, 2019, https://www.courant.com/breaking-news/hc-news-new-britain-stewart-insult-20191021-rdeurr7sl-jgezeao5earcsfwai-story.html

**Hartford Courant:** Don Stacom, *Hartford Courant*, "At inauguration, New Britain Mayor Erin Stewart makes plea for an end to social media sniping and insults from all sides," November 12, 2019, https://www.courant.com/community/new-britain/hc-news-new-britain-inauguration-20191112-lccteflq4jfa3c3bemldqij2me-story.html

**New Britain Herald:** Catherine Shen, *New Britain Herald,* "Mayor Erin Stewart urges civility, cooperation at her inauguration," November 12, 2019, http://www.newbritainherald.com/NBH-New+Britain+News/361529/mayor-erin-stewart-urges-civility-cooperation-at-her-inauguration

Made in the USA
Monee, IL
15 September 2020